WORLD'S SCARIEST PLACES

CENTENNIAL BOOKS

CENTENNIAL BOOKS

WORLD'S SCARIEST PLACES

Haunted · Creepy · Abandoned

MICHAEL FLEEMAN

WORLD'S

SCARIEST PLACES

EERILY EMPTY
Łapalice Castle in
Poland was never
fully finished.

REAL-LIFE HAUNTS

The world is full of some frightfully good sights—
just be sure to bring your courage along with your passport.

Go ahead, open that rusty gate. We dare you. What's the worst that could happen? They've all been dead for a century. As you wander through that ancient cemetery, your pulse quickens and a bead of cold sweat dribbles down the back of your neck. You fight a war with your imagination. Has that dark figure always been there? Did that tombstone just move? When you feel a poke in the ribs and a warm breath against your cheek, you know it's time to run for your life.

You have entered a place where the senses obliterate all logic, the basic rules of physics no longer apply and that yawning gap between the living and the dead is filled with everything you most fear. These are the sites where the bones jangle, the cries go unheeded, the walls tremble, the vines creepy-crawl, the wind whispers with pain and the blood never stops running. These are the world's scariest places.

In this international visitor's guide to the macabre, the melancholy and the merely terrifying, you'll descend into the cool, dark underworld of hollow-eyed mummies dressed in their military finest in Sicily's Catacombs of the Capuchins. Marvel at the sparkling thousand-year-old bones that still lie in the Cave of the Crystal Sepulchre in Belize. Or hunt ghosts in Union Cemetery in Connecticut, where the mysterious White Lady has been spotted by a husband-and-wife team of paranormal investigators.

In Philadelphia, Eastern State Penitentiary's solitary cells are so suffocating they made no less a hardened criminal than Al Capone cower. The sad handprint of a desperate patient at Australia's Beechworth Lunatic Asylum remains pressed on the wall. And a "shadow person" resembling a doctor in a smock makes his lonely nightly rounds at Waverly Hills Sanatorium for tuberculosis in Kentucky.

The towering Romanian castle that may have inspired the gothic novel *Dracula* invites visitors to spend Halloween night sleeping (or not) in a coffin. In England, tourists hoping to see the Crown Jewels may instead get a rude greeting by the ghost of Anne Boleyn, minus her royal head.

Crime fanatics will be fascinated by the murder houses where Lizzie Borden took an ax to her father and stepmother and where Charles Manson's followers slaughtered in the name of the "family." And pop culture warriors will never know what's going to pop up at the real-life New Jersey summer camp that inspired the *Friday the 13th* movies or in the actual Colorado hotel that spurred Stephen King to write *The Shining*.

If after all this you crave fresh air and solitude, don't get anywhere near the Suicide Forest of Japan, where you might just stumble over a dead body, or Mexico's Island of the Dolls, where Ken and Barbie–and thousands of their friends–dangle from the trees. And especially stay away from abandoned Pripyat in the Ukraine, where bad memories (and radiation) linger from the Chernobyl nuclear disaster.

It's a global tour that's guaranteed to make your skin crawl and fray your nerves. You'll probably come home in one piece—but check that luggage for stowaways just to be sure.

—*Michael Fleeman*

DEAD & BURIED

THE DEARLY DEPARTED DRIFT AMONG THE LIVING IN THESE TERRIFYING CEMETERIES, CATACOMBS AND HOUSES OF BONES.

PALERMO, ITALY

CATACOMBS OF THE CAPUCHINS

Mummies that look hauntingly alive in full dress populate this macabre underground world.

Stare into the gruesome face of death, and death stares back. In this freakish vault of preserved bodies with hollow eyes, religious men, professionals and even children are dressed as if at any moment they'll celebrate mass, command troops or awaken from a nap.

The Catacombs of the Capuchins may be the most terrifying place on Earth, or the most fascinating, depending on your relationship with mummies.

In the late 16th century, when the Capuchin monastery's cemetery ran out of room, the monks started digging. Two years later, the catacombs were ready, and 45 remains were exhumed from the cemetery for transfer. That's when the monks made a startling discovery: Many of the bodies had not decomposed. They had instead naturally mummified and were so well-preserved that the monks could recognize some of their brothers' faces.

This message from God made the monks resolve to preserve all of the bodies for the new Catacombs of the Capuchins, on the outskirts of Palermo, and display them like religious relics in the clothing and other adornments they wore in life. Mummification retained the skin and hair, and even their mustaches. In this most bizarre realm, where the living interact with the dead, some 8,000 bodies can be found—1,200 of them mummies.

Dead friars are dressed in their vestments, robes and ropes worn as a penance. Local notables—political officials, military officers, surgeons and sculptors—are wearing clothing specified in their wills. One French colonel from the 1800s was buried in full French Bourbon uniform, his bony hands clasped in front of him. Some had their garments regularly changed. Families would come and visit their departed loved ones, praying with them, holding their hands.

Bodies hang from hooks on the walls and lie in glass-enclosed coffins. Two children share a rocking chair. Those whose families couldn't afford special placement rest on shelves. Class distinctions followed them in formaldehyde to death. The catacombs segregate the remains by male, female, priests, monks, children, professionals and virgins. Their skins tight against their skulls, they appear to be laughing hysterically— or screaming out of horror.

DEATH WALLS
Mummies hang from hooks or lie in alcoves.

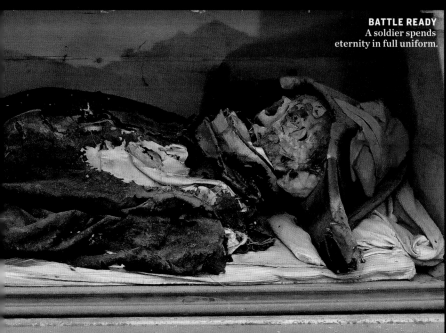

BATTLE READY
A soldier spends eternity in full uniform.

Do the Eyes of a Baby Mummy Blink?

In her glass-paned coffin, Rosalia Lombardo, who died of pneumonia in 1920 at age 2, appears to be peacefully asleep, her blond curls tied in a ribbon, until she cracks open her eyes, a phenomenon visitors have photographed. Unlike the other bodies, which were essentially dried out, Rosalia was preserved with a process using formaldehyde and water, plus zinc to keep her rigid, making her look hauntingly lifelike—but not alive. Catacombs officials insist that the changing light plays tricks.

PARIS, FRANCE

PARIS CATACOMBS

Make a date with the dead in the "carrières de Paris" deep below France's capital city.

Beneath the City of Light lurks a world of darkness, a maze of tunnels and rooms filled with the bones from 6 million Parisians that are arranged into macabre sculptures, piled high into walls and stuffed into every nook and cranny of the limestone.

The Paris Catacombs date to the late 1700s, when flooding from heavy rains uprooted rotting corpses from the Holy Innocents cemetery, founded in the Middle Ages, forcing French authorities to find another resting place.

A defunct quarry outside the city was consecrated as the Paris Catacombs in 1786, and for decades the city's cemeteries were emptied and the bones transferred to the 57°F catacombs.

The last gruesome skeletal deposits arrived in 1859, and seven years later these 186 twisting miles of death became a tourist attraction. Graffiti dates to the French Revolution, and during World War II the French Resistance hid out in the catacombs. A portion remains open for visitors to gaze at the skulls and femurs in artistically arranged crosses, pillars and other shapes.

Bone Party

Things get weirder underground. Explorer "cataphiles" throw underground parties with booze and music. Visitors smuggle in photo gear for bizarre erotic shoots with nude models sprawled on bones. And in June 2017, two teenagers got lost for three days and suffered hypothermia before being found by rescue dogs. If you want to play by the rules, visitors can arrange for private tours that leave after 8 p.m. each evening—followed by a cocktail outside when the weather is nice. Can't make it there in person? You can view the catacombs virtually from the comfort of your (skeleton-free) home at catacombes.paris.fr.

CAYO, BELIZE

CAVE OF THE CRYSTAL SEPULCHRE

Archaeologists call it a "portal to the underworld," the place where the desperate Maya turned to human sacrifice to appease the gods.

CRYSTAL MAIDEN
A calcified skeleton sparkles in lamplight.

The ancient Maya called it the "place of fright," the pitch-black home of monsters with names like Stabbing Demon and Flying Scab. When drought gripped the land, wilted the crops and starved the people, the despondent Maya ventured through the portal into the underworld, their crude torches throwing eerie shadows against the cave walls, as they made offerings to Chac, god of rain.

Today, adventurers can explore the ominous world once called Xibalba and now known as the Actun Tunichil Muknal, or Cave of the Crystal Sepulchre, where thousand-year-old human bones sparkle from calcification. Discovered in 1989, this cave—45 minutes into the jungles of the Tapir Mountain Nature Preserve in Belize—is open to tourists, as long as they travel with a government-sanctioned guide, wear no shoes and carry no cameras (two skulls were crushed by a boot and a camera).

The journey today is not much easier than it was more than a thousand years ago, when these remains were left behind as the cities of the Mayan empire collapsed, apparently due to severe drought. But because the cave is so remote, the surreal and ghastly sights inside have remained untouched for centuries.

The rocky mouth of the cave, covered by hanging vines, is accessible only by swimming through the chilly waters from the stream that runs for miles through the limestone. The waters, home to catfish and freshwater crabs, reach wading depths as the cave grows darker into the "twilight zone" of diffuse sunlight, then the "dark zones," where no light penetrates. Tiny fish nibble at explorers' legs. Giant spiders crawl up the cave walls. And time melts away.

In the first sections of the cave, the Maya left the gods ceramic pots filled with food and the blood of animals. Deeper in the dark zones can be found the bones from 14 human sacrifices, including the remains of seven children, one of whom was 1 year old. Many of the bones show signs of violence: crushed skulls, dismemberment, nicks in the ribs suggesting disembowelment. One teen appears to have been bound before death. A ladder leads up to the small room where the Crystal Maiden, one of the most famous skeletons in the world, has lain for more than 1,000 years. Once thought to be the remains of a teenage girl, they are now believed to be those of a man of about 20. Two crushed vertebrae suggest the person died from clubbing, perhaps in this very spot.

Do the Dead Speak?

The TV show *Ghost Hunters International* visited Actun Tunichil Muknal to find out whether those sacrificed to the gods had anything to say. The team's electronic devices began to register as if somebody was trying to communicate with them, and they did pick up some sounds on their recorder.

WRONG ADDRESS
Are all the
bodies in their
rightful places?

WOONSOCKET, RHODE ISLAND

PRECIOUS BLOOD CEMETERY

After the floodwaters rose and the bodies floated away, the dead came back as ghosts.

In 1955, back-to-back hurricanes slammed into the northeastern U.S. Just a week after Hurricane Connie pounded the region, Hurricane Diana arrived with winds topping 115 mph and rainfall of up to 10 inches.

Floodwaters swelled the Blackstone River and Harris Pond in Woonsocket, and a torrent swept through Precious Blood Cemetery. More than 50 coffins were uprooted and floated downstream, scattering human remains. When the water receded, the bodies were transferred to a mausoleum and placed in new caskets under new markers. But legend has it that not all the remains were returned correctly. Today, the ghosts of those displaced corpses are said to return to Precious Blood seeking their rightful final resting places.

Closed to new burials since 1955, the cemetery has an eerie feel, particularly when the fog drifts in from the ocean. With parts of the grounds stretching into neighboring Massachusetts, Precious Blood Cemetery has impressive and imposing crypts and tombstones as well as crumbling old markers and simple crosses, some with the names of the dead handwritten on them.

HANGING COFFINS

The dead hover above the forest in caskets dangling from cliffs.

High above the jungles of Luzon Island in the northern Philippines, the dead dangle for dear afterlife. For centuries, the indigenous Igorots of Sagada Echo Valley have squeezed corpses into tiny coffins hanging from the walls of sheer cliffs.

This bizarre tableau has become an attraction for many tourists, who trek 12 miles by bus from Manila (longer in the rainy season, when floods and avalanches wipe out the crude roads) to gaze at the hanging coffins of Sagada. The more disrespectful visitors have broken into coffins or stolen bones that fall to the ground.

Though not as common today, for the Igorots, the practice was part of a longstanding sacred ritual that began before death, when the elderly carved their own coffins out of a single log. If they were too weak from age or illness, a son or another relative performed the task.

At death, bodies were wrapped in a blanket and rattan leaves, then squeezed into the coffin in the fetal position, representing how they were carried in their mother's womb. Once, the caskets were only 3 feet long, so the bones had to be cracked to make the body fit.

The coffin was sealed with vines, then transported in a procession. Touching a drop of blood from the departed was considered good luck

The coffins then were raised up the cliff and placed in caves or crevices or affixed to the cliff wall with nails or ropes. There the remains would stay for generations.

Igorots believed that the more a person was loved in life, the higher they'd be placed in death. But some other reasons for the elevated graves are more practical: to protect the corpses from rotting in the damp soil, from animals or even from ancient headhunters. Others have suggested the ritual preserved valuable land for planting crops.

The custom continues, though now the coffins are built twice as long to avoid the grisly bone-breaking, and the country's new generations of Christians have left the practice to a dwindling number of elders, with only one

SKY BURIAL
Coffins are hung from, or bolted to, the cliff.

casket raised every couple of years. "It's a tradition that is slowly coming to an end," tribal elder Soledad Belingom says in the *Rough Guide to the Philippines*. "It's dying out."

A Chinese Import?

Coffins dating to 1000 B.C. have been discovered in southern China, where the Bo people believed a high-altitude entombment brought peace to the deceased. A leading theory holds that thousands of years ago, Malayo-Polynesians migrated to the Philippines from Taiwan, whose people had come from China's mainland. Though no evidence links the hanging coffins to the two cultures, there have been discoveries in the Philippines of ancient artifacts made from jade that are believed to have originated in Taiwan, 300 miles to the north, in the China Sea.

"Cliff-hanging coffins supposedly kept their occupants closer to heaven."
Reuters

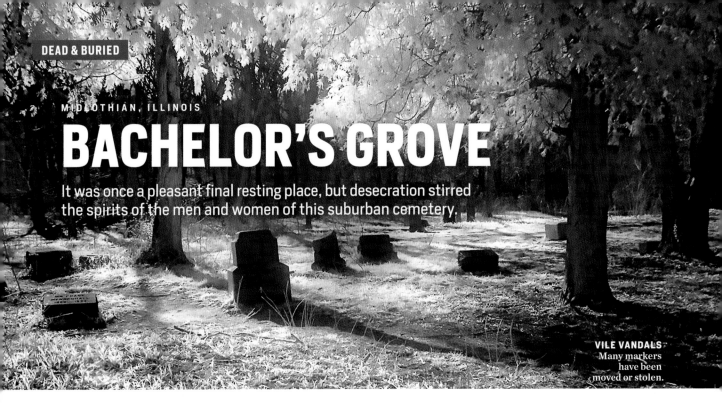

MIDLOTHIAN, ILLINOIS

BACHELOR'S GROVE

It was once a pleasant final resting place, but desecration stirred the spirits of the men and women of this suburban cemetery.

VILE VANDALS Many markers have been moved or stolen.

B achelor's Grove Cemetery first came to the nation's attention in 1934 when Robert Ripley featured it in his nationally syndicated illustrated "Believe It or Not!" column, exclaiming, "Women are buried in Bachelor's Grove Cemetery."

Better believe it. Locals had long known about this 1-acre plot where dozens of people—men and women—were buried in the 19th century when this Chicago suburb was still a wild Western country that drew settlers from the East. The source of the name is in dispute. Unmarried male immigrants from England may have in fact been the first buried here. The name may also be a variation of a German family name.

Either way, for much of its existence, the ghosts seemed to stay away. Long-abandoned by the 1930s, Bachelor's Grove was a popular picnic spot for families during the day and a place of morbid curiosity at night. No evening at the dance hall was complete without men bringing their dates to the cemetery to scare them before trying to get frisky.

BELIEVE The original column about the cemetery by Robert Ripley

Today, Bachelor's Grove holds another kind of reputation: It is widely considered one of the most haunted cemeteries in America. "In all my years of paranormal research and investigation, there is no single place at which I have documented more ostensibly paranormal activity and collected more reports of such than Bachelor's Grove," writes local historian/paranormal researcher Ursula Bielski in *Haunted Bachelor's Grove*.

The cemetery is located at the end of a lonely road, and visitors tell stories of strange lights, phantom dogs, compasses and GPS devices that go haywire, and specters of all sorts: robed figures, a man with a lantern, a farmer with his plow horse and, most famous, The Woman in White, also called the Madonna of Bachelor's Grove, who purportedly was photographed in 1991 sitting on a broken headstone (see box, right).

END OF THE ROAD
Once a lovers' lane, it now offers different thrills.

HOURS SUNRISE TO SUNSET

CLOSED

BACHELOR'S GROVE CEMETERY

NO MAN'S LAND
Despite the name, women do populate—and haunt—the cemetery.

"A lot of people stay away from the Grove because of the strange pull."
Ursula Bielski, author of
Haunted Bachelor's Grove

The tales began in relatively recent decades. From the 1950s through the 1970s, the cemetery fell prey to vandals who toppled, moved and stole gravestones and covered them with graffiti. Some dared to dig up remains and take off with the buried bones. Satanic rituals sometimes took place at a nearby pond, and chickens and other animals were sacrificed.

The desecration created an ominous setting—and, some believe, stirred up the spirits. Though one of countless little graveyards, Bachelor's Grove stands out among others for its many reports of paranormal activity and the fascination it continues to hold.

Who Is She?
They call her the Madonna of Bachelor's Grove or The Woman in White. This sad spirit wanders amid the tombstones, usually at night under a full moon, looking for her little sister's marker, which is missing. In her arms she holds a swaddled baby. She is the most famous specter of the cemetery, and this 1991 photo by paranormal researcher Jude Huff allegedly captured her on a tombstone.

NORTH LONDON, ENGLAND

HIGHGATE CEMETERY

Does a vampire lurk amid the cracked
headstones and mossy mausoleums?

ROOM FOR GLOOM
Abandoned by people, the
cemetery was overtaken
by the natural and, some
say, supernatural.

INSPIRATION
Novels, films, even video games have been set in Highgate.

WILD THINGS
Trees and shrubs have grown and thrived without human intervention.

FADED GLORY
London's elite once vied for the best final resting places.

"A secluded funerary at its most evocative."
Friends of Highgate Cemetery

During the Victorian era, it was the place to be—and be buried. Frightened by tales of body snatchers stealing the dead from London's public graveyards, in 1839 members of the city's high society established the private Highgate Cemetery. There, they competed to erect the most elaborate headstones and the most lavish neo-Gothic tombs and mausoleums. In this oasis of beauty, rest and status, trees and wildflowers flourished and foxes scampered among the tombstones of luminaries like novelist George Eliot, philosopher Karl Marx and the parents of Charles Dickens. A plot in Highgate proved to the world that your dearly departed had arrived.

But by World War II, the 20-acre grounds had seen better days. Neglect and unforgiving weather had left the tombstones, crypts and mausoleums in ruins. In the early 1960s, Highgate was abandoned and locked, and the cemetery was left to the elements, wildlife, vandals and, some say, beings from beyond.

Stories of ghosts, demons, dark-robed spirits and a ghoul with blazing red eyes spread like the once-trimmed vines now growing wild. Then on a Friday the 13th in 1970, a full-fledged panic ensued when the ITV network aired interviews with purported witnesses to a vampire roaming the deteriorating cemetery.

People descended on Highgate, scaling the walls in the hopes of getting a glimpse of the Highgate Vampire. It was a crisis for which the quiet community was ill-equipped, and many blamed Hollywood: The horror movies *The Body Beneath* and *Taste the Blood of Dracula* had been filmed on location in Highgate

that year. "This ancient and unspoiled area of North London is believed by many to be one of the most haunted locations in the U.K.," wrote *Haunted Highgate* author Della Farrant.

This rankles Friends of Highgate, a charity trust created to rescue the cemetery from disrepair. According to its website, the Friends celebrate Highgate as "one of England's greatest treasures" and home to "some of the finest funerary architecture in the country."

When a photographer snapped a picture of what he thought could be the ghost of a Victorian-era nurse in 2012, the Friends fired back. "There are no ghosts here at all," the trust's chief executive, Ian Dungavell, told the *Hampstead & Highgate Express*. "Highgate Cemetery is a place of quiet reflection for people in mourning." Tell it to the vampire.

EASTON, CONNECTICUT

UNION CEMETERY

A Hollywood ghost hunter popularizes this historic graveyard where spirits float and eyes blaze red.

THEY'RE WATCHING
The White Lady has company—a spirit named Red Eyes.

A t the junction of routes 59 and 136 in Easton, Connecticut, next to Easton Baptist Church, is Union Cemetery, which first opened in the early 1700s and gets its spooky reputation from one red-eyed spirit, one ghost and two famous ghost hunters.

Red Eyes is said to live in the woods behind the graveyard, its eyes glowing crimson. Even more eerie is the White Lady, who is said to walk amid the grave markers, her long black hair and white gown flowing behind her. She has also been known to wander onto Route 59, where terrified drivers plow straight through her.

Hearing reports of the White Lady were Ed and Lorraine Warren, husband-and-wife paranormal investigators whose exploits inspired the movie *The Conjuring* and its sequel, starring Patrick Wilson and Vera Farmiga as the couple.

One hot night in September 1990, Ed parked his van outside the cemetery and set up his camcorder on a tripod, hoping

GHOST HUNTERS
Ed and Lorraine Warren

to capture the ghost. At 2:40 a.m., he heard a woman weeping. "I could see all these ghost lights suddenly forming into a figure of a woman," Ed said in an interview with the show *Seekers of the Supernatural.* "This huge shadow ghost pushed her toward Route 59, and that was it."

As quickly as she appeared, she was gone. But Ed insists he captured her on video. Though he's shown footage to people privately, including to Steven Novella

of Skeptic Blog, who said, "a provocative shape can be seen, but no details which would aid definitive identification," neither Ed or Lorraine (both of whom are now deceased) ever produced the video for independent scientific examination.

The White Lady tale, reports of seeing Red Eyes and the popularity of *The Conjuring* have made the cemetery so popular that police have had to close it after dark.

ST. LOUIS CEMETERY NO. 1

The spookiest cemetery in the South is ruled by the spirit of a Voodoo Queen.

In the counterculture classic film *Easy Rider,* Dennis Hopper and Peter Fonda rumble into a cemetery for a hallucinogenic encounter with the dead, grateful and otherwise. No doubt about it, New Orleans' St. Louis Cemetery No. 1 is a trip. Eight blocks from the Mississippi River, this 200-year-old block-size burial ground holds 700 souls in a maze of crumbling crypts and chipped headstones. That statue a blitzed-out Fonda talks to? You'll find it atop the Italian Benevolent Society Tomb.

St. Louis No. 1, one of three nearby graveyards operated by the Catholic diocese, has earned its reputation as one of the most famous cemeteries in the world for more than its Hollywood past (it was also featured in *Interview With a Vampire*). Stroll along the narrow cobblestone pathways at night, and you'll hear more than your feet crunching on the broken shells from Lake Pontchartrain. Some insist you'll also hear the wails and groans of ghosts.

The many spirits are said to include an old man perched on a tomb and even a ghost who delivers flowers. But the most famous is the ghost of Marie Laveau, the legendary turbaned Voodoo Queen of New Orleans. Upper-crust society flocked to Laveau in the 1800s to hear their fortunes, buy her charms and betray their secrets. Wearing her colorful clothes and signature turban as she walks between the gravestones, Laveau's ghost can be cranky, pinching or scratching anybody who doesn't believe in voodoo.

So popular is Laveau in death that her tomb has been repeatedly desecrated over the years. After somebody painted it pink in 2013, the diocese ponied up $10,000 for restoration and eventually closed the entire graveyard to the public, allowing only tours with contracted guides.

CITY OF THE DEAD
Located below sea level, the cemetery keeps the corpses above ground.

TOMBSTONE, ARIZONA

BOOTHILL GRAVEYARD

They died with their boots on. Now they stroll this
Old West cemetery known for its frontier humor.

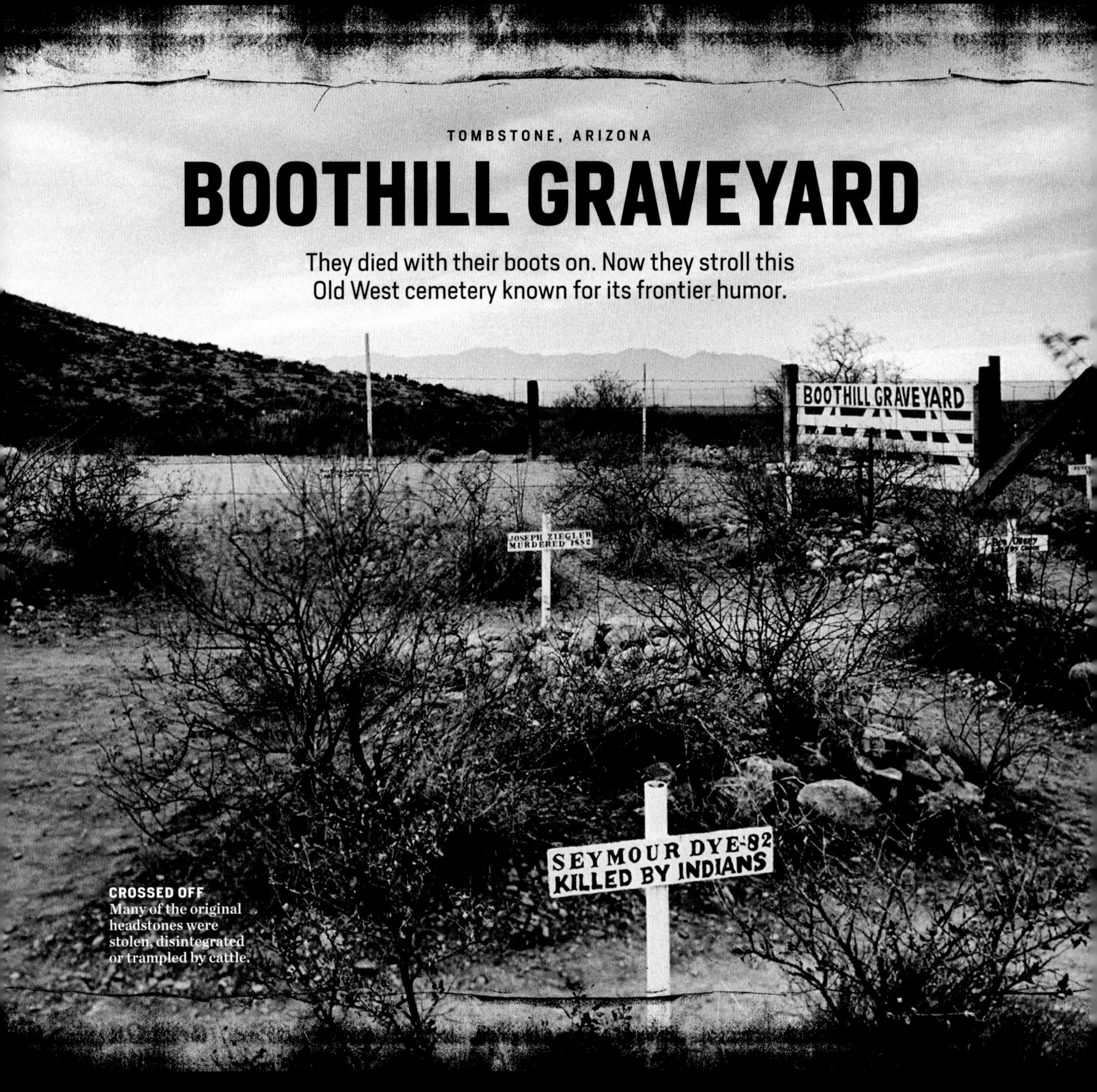

BOOTHILL GRAVEYARD

JOSEPH ZIEGLER
MURDERED 1882

SEYMOUR DYE 82
KILLED BY INDIANS

CROSSED OFF
Many of the original
headstones were
stolen, disintegrated
or trampled by cattle.

Boothill Graveyard greets death with a cockeyed grin. A famous marker in this cemetery above the historic town of Tombstone, Arizona, reads: "Here lies Lester Moore. Four slugs from a .44. No Les. No More."

Established in 1879, Boothill Graveyard represents the prototypical Wild West cemetery—gritty and eccentric. Its name has been replicated in burial grounds outside countless mining towns and in the TV show *Gunsmoke*, and its spirits are said to mingle with the tourists.

This original Boothill is the final resting place for people of myth and movies, outlaws and outsiders, including Dutch Annie, the popular madam known as the "Queen of the Red Light District," and the many men who died with their boots on, among them three victims of the infamous 1881 shoot-out at the O.K. Corral.

The markers, many re-created from the original wood ones that disintegrated, are well-known for their frontier humor, like this classic: "Here lies George Johnson. Hanged by mistake 1882. He was right. We was wrong. But we strung him up and now he's gone."

Others memorialize the circumstances of death. "Found dead in his cabin with bullet wounds," reads one. "Died in a dispute," reads another. Some simply have one-word descriptions: "Hanged" (and "Legally Hanged," there being a distinction back in the day). One marker shouts in capital letters: "MURDERED."

The cemetery also speaks to the realities of the Old West rarely seen in movies, such as the division between races, even in death. Nearly 100 of the 300 dead were buried without names, many because they were Chinese immigrants. A separate lot was set aside for Jews.

It's perhaps inevitable that so much violence brings out the ghosts. Guests report seeing doomed Billy Clanton, gunned down at the O.K. Corral, drifting back toward town. Other unrecognizable figures appear as shadows or mist, and some insist they've seen human forms poking their heads out from behind the tombstones.

And for more ghostly intrigue, check out the town's renowned Bird Cage Theater, a bullet-ravaged building with a history of paranormal activity.

DRAWING CROWDS More than 140,000 people visit the graveyard each year for the history and the rough-hewn humor.

"Boot hill, boot hill. So cold, so still."

Lyrics to "Gunfight at the O.K. Corral"

NO JUSTICE
The Salem Witch Trials led to the execution of 20 people—14 of them women—most by hanging.

SALEM, MASSACHUSETTS

HOWARD STREET CEMETERY

A ghost from the Salem Witch Trials avenges his suffering by returning to his killing field.

During the hysteria of the Salem Witch Trials, an 80-year-old man named Giles Corey stood accused of evildoings by 19-year-old Mercy Lewis. "I verily believe in my heart that Giles Corey is a dreadful wizard," the teen said in a 1692 deposition.

The principled and stubborn Corey, whose wife was also accused of witchcraft, would not dignify this claim with a denial. After being charged, he refused even to enter a plea.

His insolence got him the draconian sentence of "pressing," in which he was stripped naked and forced to lie under a wooden door weighted down with heavy rocks.

Two days into the torture, the sheriff taunted him: "Do you confess?"

"Damn you, sheriff!" Corey replied. "I curse you and Salem."

Corey finally succumbed after three days of this treatment, but his death would reverberate long afterward through history.

His defiance is seen as a turning point that "tended to awaken the people to a realization of the grave responsibility resting on them as a Christian community," reports the book, *A Historical Sketch of Salem 1626–1879.*

What's more, Corey got his revenge. According to legend, a string of local sheriffs would suffer the "curse of Giles Corey" by either dying in office or being forced to resign from their duties due to heart ailments.

As for Corey, he is said to have never departed the field where he was killed. He reportedly returned to the grounds as a ghost after they were turned into the Howard Street Cemetery in 1801, to remind people of the great pain and injustice he endured.

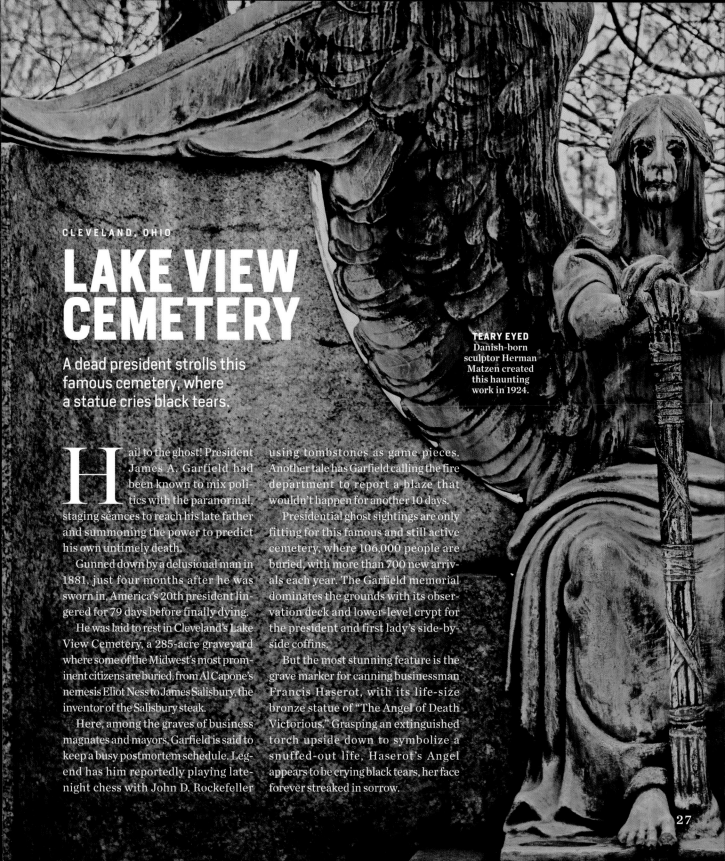

CLEVELAND, OHIO

LAKE VIEW CEMETERY

A dead president strolls this
famous cemetery, where
a statue cries black tears.

TEARY EYED
Danish-born
sculptor Herman
Matzen created
this haunting
work in 1924.

Hail to the ghost! President James A. Garfield had been known to mix politics with the paranormal, staging séances to reach his late father and summoning the power to predict his own untimely death.

Gunned down by a delusional man in 1881, just four months after he was sworn in, America's 20th president lingered for 79 days before finally dying.

He was laid to rest in Cleveland's Lake View Cemetery, a 285-acre graveyard where some of the Midwest's most prominent citizens are buried, from Al Capone's nemesis Eliot Ness to James Salisbury, the inventor of the Salisbury steak.

Here, among the graves of business magnates and mayors, Garfield is said to keep a busy postmortem schedule. Legend has him reportedly playing late-night chess with John D. Rockefeller

using tombstones as game pieces. Another tale has Garfield calling the fire department to report a blaze that wouldn't happen for another 10 days.

Presidential ghost sightings are only fitting for this famous and still active cemetery, where 106,000 people are buried, with more than 700 new arrivals each year. The Garfield memorial dominates the grounds with its observation deck and lower-level crypt for the president and first lady's side-by-side coffins.

But the most stunning feature is the grave marker for canning businessman Francis Haserot, with its life-size bronze statue of "The Angel of Death Victorious." Grasping an extinguished torch upside down to symbolize a snuffed-out life, Haserot's Angel appears to be crying black tears, her face forever streaked in sorrow.

27

CREEPIEST CHURCHES

These once-hallowed halls of religion now lie in ruins but continue to attract onlookers seeking the realm of spirits.

VILLERS-LA-VILLE, BELGIUM
VILLERS ABBEY

A visitor feels closer to heaven at the ruins of Belgium's Villers Abbey—and not just because there are no roofs anymore. Founded in 1146 and built up over decades in the 13th century—it took some 70 years to complete—the complex is surrounded by 100 acres of forests and pastures in Villers-la-Ville. At its peak, it housed 100 monks and 300 lay brothers. In the 1500s, the abbey began a slow decline due to war, financial problems and a dwindling supply of monks. The French Revolution doomed it for good.

Abandoned in 1796, it decayed further when a rail line cut through the property in 1855. Conservation efforts and historic designation have preserved the ruins. The graceful Cistercian-style vaults, arches and rose windows now provide a dramatic setting for picnics, festivals and quiet contemplation. The abbey also has a meditative pathway that encourages visitors to relax as they walk through a scented garden.

ST. GEORGE'S CHURCH

When the roof collapsed during a funeral in 1968, the congregation was so terrified that this 600-year-old church was haunted they refused to return. Thieves broke into the abandoned building and took off with statues, paintings, even the clock from the tower; vandals and years of neglect have also taken their toll. To draw attention to the church and raise money for restoration, a sculptor named Jakub Hadrava created 32 statues of ghosts draped in white sheets and placed them in the pews. The haunting exhibit now has drawn waves of visitors who leave donations to make repairs.

GARY, INDIANA
CITY METHODIST CHURCH

The nine-story English Gothic church opened in 1926 with stained glass windows, soaring pillars and carved stonework, plus a music studio, cafeteria, gym and 1,000-seat hall. Half of the $1 million cost—$14 million today—was covered by U.S. Steel. The church had 2,000 congregants in its 1950s heyday. But as the steel industry lagged, so did the city. In the 1960s, economic decline shrank membership; the church was left vacant in 1975 and soon fell into disrepair.

MAGELANG, INDONESIA
CHICKEN CHURCH

Daniel Alamsjah followed a vision from God to build a house of prayer that looked like a dove, and started constructing a bird-shaped place of worship in a mountain forest on the Indonesian island of Java. Opening its doors in the 1990s even before it was finished, the church welcomed all faiths.

Unfortunately, Alamsjah's pious devotion was not matched by equal artistic or architectural talents, and the structure looks more like a giant angry chicken than a dove. With a huge squawking beak and feathers over the entrance, Gereja Ayam, or Chicken Church as the locals call it, ran into financial problems in 2000 and was vacated; it now attracts curious visitors.

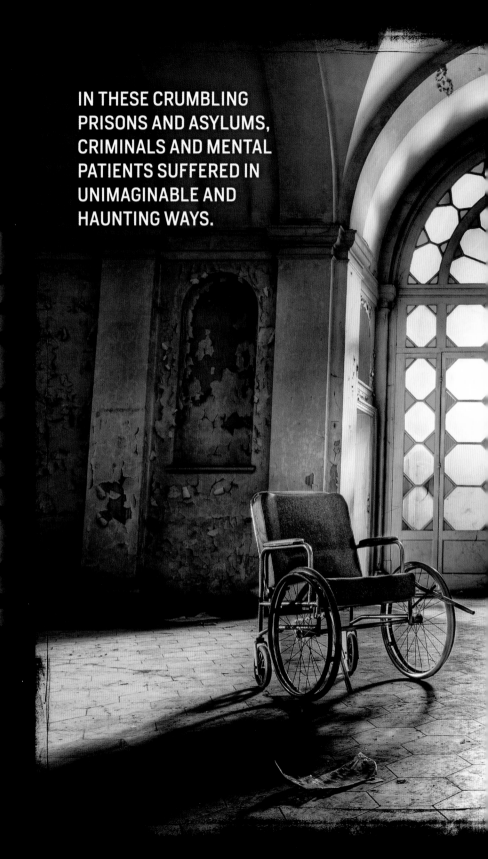

INSTITUTIONAL HORRORS

IN THESE CRUMBLING PRISONS AND ASYLUMS, CRIMINALS AND MENTAL PATIENTS SUFFERED IN UNIMAGINABLE AND HAUNTING WAYS.

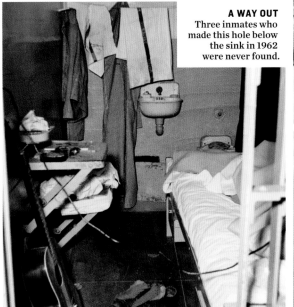

A WAY OUT
Three inmates who made this hole below the sink in 1962 were never found.

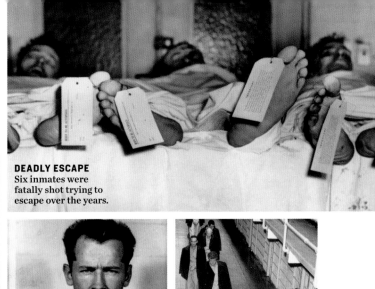

DEADLY ESCAPE
Six inmates were fatally shot trying to escape over the years.

FAMOUS CONS
Black Mass gangster Whitey Bulger served four years.

SAN FRANCISCO, CALIFORNIA

ALCATRAZ

Voices, clanking metal and even music linger long after the last inmates have left.

As the sun sets and the fog rolls in through the Golden Gate, a chill descends upon the tiny island. The old cell blocks where the worst of society were holed up behind bars in 8-by-4 enclosures seem to rattle to life. Was that a moan of despair—or the howl of the wind? A shadow or a ghost? By morning, it hardly matters. One night in Alcatraz can turn skeptics into believers.

So many stories of strange, mysterious events swirl around the Alcatraz Federal Penitentiary that it has earned The Rock the title of the world's most haunted prison, if not most haunted place. "It hasn't been operational since 1963," *New York* magazine observed in 1996, "but Alcatraz remains ultra-sinister, perversely fascinating, iconic."

Once shunned by Native Americans who feared evil spirits on the island, the site became a fort—archaeologists discovered still-intact Civil War-era buildings and tunnels underneath the prison, which opened in 1934. In its nearly 50-year history, it saw eight murders by inmates, including one of a guard. Five prisoners also took their own lives and another dozen died trying to escape.

Hardened guards who had initially laughed off inmates' scary tales would report ghostly brushes against the back of the neck, the sounds of chains from empty cells, and visions of Native Americans who died during the Civil War era. An entire lighthouse was said to have emerged from the fog—and vanished.

Sightings intensified after the prison shut down. While a bustling tourist attraction during the day, night brings out the haunts: the screech of a swinging cell door in C Block where an inmate was murdered; voices in D Block; whispers; and notes from a harmonica and a banjo.

HARD TIME
"You break the rules, you go to prison. You break the prison rules, you go to Alcatraz," reads a sign at the main entrance.

GOD'S LIGHT
Skylights—intended to bring divine illumination—could not pierce the darkness within.

PHILADELPHIA, PENNSYLVANIA

EASTERN STATE PENITENTIARY

A ghostly guard stands watch, and an eerie cold grips the cell blocks where the worst once walked.

When Al Capone arrived at Eastern State Penitentiary in 1929 to serve his first federal time, the gangster got the kind of special treatment he'd come to expect due to his money and notoriety. His cell featured Oriental rugs, a lamp, a cabinet radio, a fancy desk and upholstered chairs. An oil painting hung over his bed. But over the next eight months, the notorious crime boss would find that no amount of jailhouse luxury would spare him the terrors within this prison's stone walls.

At night, guards would hear Capone screaming in fright, begging a man he called "Jimmy" to go away. A check of the cell would turn up nobody but a rattled Capone. It seemed the nocturnal visitor was Albert Kachellek, aka James "Jimmy" Clark, the second in command of Capone's rival gang. There was no way he could have snuck into the prison: Clark had been killed just three months earlier in the St. Valentine's Day massacre ordered by Capone.

In Eastern State Penitentiary every cell was single occupancy. When moved, the inmates had their heads shrouded so they couldn't interact with other prisoners. The theory was that alone time would allow self-reflection for one's transgressions. But solitary confinement also drove prisoners crazy.

Built in 1829, Eastern State Penitentiary still stands, a fortress with vaulted ceilings. A place where untold numbers of prisoners died in violence and suicide, and many more from disease, Eastern State inflicted its most severe punishment on the mind. The spirits, some believe, have not forgotten.

There are reports of shadows darting across the catwalks, wild temperature swings and the sounds of laughter and whispers. Others have seen the image of a prison guard still standing watch in the tower. And many report eerie feelings of being watched by something. Even seasoned guides admit to events that can't be explained—a movement over there, a sound over here—leaving plenty of room to wonder.

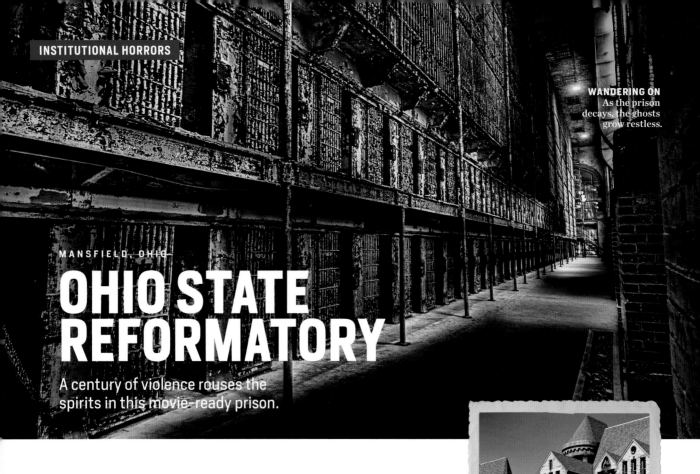

WANDERING ON
As the prison decays, the ghosts grow restless.

MANSFIELD, OHIO

OHIO STATE REFORMATORY

A century of violence rouses the spirits in this movie-ready prison.

When producers needed a location for shooting the gritty prison drama *The Shawshank Redemption*, they went to the Ohio State Reformatory, a historic lockup that squeezed 154,000 inmates into tight cells over 94 highly turbulent years.

Built from 1886 to 1910, this Romanesque castle-like edifice was originally intended as a place where mostly lower-security first-time offenders could be taught new skills to make them ready to contribute to society.

But by the 1960s, the reformatory had been rechristened the Mansfield Correctional Institute and stuffed with hardened criminals. When the courts finally forced its closure in 1990 for deplorable conditions, Mansfield had become a symbol of a broken penal system, valued only as a Hollywood set.

Over the next decades, the prison grounds deteriorated, the cells holding only bad memories and the spirits of desperate men.

As the BBC observed in a program on Mansfield, "It's a place where the ghosts of abused inmates and staff with heavy consciences roam the halls, moving equipment and slamming doors."

The human toll can be seen in the reformatory's cemetery with its 215 graves, the dead identified by numbers. Inmates who didn't succumb to tuberculosis or influenza died at the hands of other inmates or by suicide, often hanging themselves with whatever they could find.

SURE SHOT
A castle of incarceration for a century.

The suffering still pulses through the decrepit site in the form of cell doors that move on their own. The angriest of the spirits have been said to punch tour guides and visitors, while some ghosts are said to float about as vague shapes—or simply exhale chilling sighs that feel like cold puffs against the cheek.

SEMARANG, INDONESIA

LAWANG SEWU

A violent past and a scary movie turn an old government building into a maze of frights.

Wartime stories of torture and executions in the basement were only the beginning. With hundreds of doorways, arches and big windows, the Lawang Sewu had been admired for its Colonial grandeur—its name translates to "1,000 doors." But the onetime headquarters of the Dutch Indies Railway Company would decay to a "dark and evidently sick" shell of its former self, left with only its nightmares and its ghosts, as the *Jakarta Post* observed in 2009.

The invading Japanese took over the Lawang Sewu during World War II, and stories proliferated about the horrors that took place in its basement prison.

DUNGEON
Prisoners were said
to be executed in this
basement prison.

After the war, the complex went to the Indonesian government, but decades of neglect left the walls cracked, the wall-

paper peeling and the outdoor spaces overtaken by weeds and rats.

Men would enter the Lawang Sewu to prove their bravery against a host of spirits: a decapitated ghost; the female vampire-like Kuntilanak; the Dutch woman who supposedly committed suicide there. A popular 2007 Indonesian movie called *Lawang Sewu: Kuntilanak's Vengeance* was set there, bringing ghost-seeking tourists.

It all amounted to a public relations nightmare for the Indonesian government, which began renovating this landmark structure as a tourist attraction in 2010 and now downplays its paranormal reputation. The only question is: Did the ghosts get the memo?

TOO QUIET
Cellblocks fell eerily silent
after the closure of this
prison, which had executed
dozens in the gas chamber.

JEFFERSON CITY, MISSOURI

MISSOURI STATE PENITENTIARY

Voices and footsteps of the
condemned return to the old prison.

For decades, it was the last stop in the criminal justice system, a metal capsule inside a small stone building, circled by a 10-foot-tall fence of chain link and razor wire. Here, the condemned would be strapped into one of two side-by-side hard metal chairs with armrests and given a lungful of toxic gas.

Forty people received the ultimate punishment at Missouri State Penitentiary from 1937 to 1989, 39 of them in the gas chamber (the 40th died by lethal injection). The maximum-security prison closed in 2004 but the chamber remains open for tours that explore the brutal history of an institution that *Time* magazine declared "America's bloodiest

47 acres." Visitors can sit in the same seat as the condemned and see their mug shots hanging on the wall, looking at you.

Constructed in 1836 as a small lockup, Missouri State Penitentiary expanded with the building of the towering A-Hall in 1868. A forbidding edifice of stone and iron bars, A-Hall held killers, kidnappers, rapists and thieves until the institution was finally shut down.

Some of history's most infamous criminals did hard time here, including gangster Charles Arthur "Pretty Boy" Floyd. The women's section held anarchist Emma Goldman for conspiracy to induce people to avoid the draft. And it was from here that James Earl Ray escaped, hiding in a box of bread being

transported to another prison, before he assassinated Martin Luther King Jr.

At one time, Missouri State had 5,300 inmates packed into decaying cells. Harsh treatment and overcrowding kept tensions high. In 1954, three days of rioting by 2,500 inmates left four of their number dead, and by the 1960s, the prison's reputation for abuse attracted scorn from activists, from the national media...and from the beyond. Inmates started hearing things that weren't there: banging and clanking, footsteps and voices. The underground dungeon cells without windows, where inmates would be left for months, received visits by ghosts and demons that some say remain to this day.

TENNESSEE STATE PRISON

The shuttered Southern institution is a popular location for filmmakers.

A fortress of punishment built by the inmates themselves, the Tennessee State Prison was overcrowded the day it opened in Nashville in 1898, with 1,400 prisoners shoved into 800 cramped cells. Conditions only got worse over its grim 94-year history.

Prisoners marched in lockstep in their striped uniforms, and spent their days toiling for up to 16 hours in convict factories for tiny wages, some of which were withheld to offset the costs of their incarceration. Nights were spent in hot, stuffy 6-by-8 cells designed for one man, but often holding as many as four.

The worst of the worst came here, including James Earl Ray, who assassinated Dr. Martin Luther King Jr. When prisoners weren't rioting or setting fires, they were trying to escape by any means possible: blowing out a wall in 1902; smashing a prison rail line locomotive through the gate in 1907. After a class-action lawsuit alleging harsh conditions, the prison was closed in 1992, with an injunction preventing it from ever being used for inmates again.

TWISTED UP
The prison, which was used to film *The Green Mile* (above) and *Walk the Line*, suffered severe structural damages from a tornado in March 2020.

ESSEX COUNTY JAIL

A decaying way station for criminals faces the wrecking ball despite its long history.

It's a nightmare you'd think nobody would ever want to revisit, a bleak old crumbling complex of cavernous cell-blocks once stuffed to overflowing with hundreds of inmates awaiting their fates in court. Behind it once loomed the gallows where murderers were hanged.

For more than 130 years, the Old Essex County Jail served as the county's primary lockup, until its doors clanked shut for the last time in 1970. Serving next as the local headquarters for the Bureau of Narcotics Control,

the facility was finally declared too decrepit for any kind of use.

Abandoned and left to ruin, the jail was ravaged by time, the bars rusting, the paint peeling, the ceilings collapsing. Taggers added graffiti to the sad messages left by inmates. Spike Lee filmed scenes from *Malcolm X* here.

And yet they came back, the same sorts of people—drug addicts, dealers and petty criminals—that once passed through this facility. Now homeless squatters occupy those same cells.

Decried as an unsafe eyesore, the old jail was targeted for demolition by the

city of Newark. But resistance rose up from those who still considered it worth saving.

Preservationists called Essex County Jail, built in 1837 and expanded over the decades, a decaying tribute to its creator, John Haviland, America's leading architect of jails and penitentiaries who also designed New York City's infamous "The Tombs."

As Matt Gosser of Newark's Preservation & Landmarks Committee told *The Star-Ledger*, "You can still bring people on tours in here and people can get a sense of the history."

> ## "Old Essex County Jail remains a sinister and forbidding place."
> ### *The New York Times*

NO HOPE One inmate left a message on a wall: "Where Evil Dwells II."

LONG DECAY
At more than
180 years old,
the jail has been
abandoned for
50 years.

41

IONE, CALIFORNIA

PRESTON CASTLE

The ghost of a bludgeoned housekeeper haunts this castle for bad boys.

"Life was tough here."
Donnie Page, Castle docent

When boys went bad they would be sent to the Preston School of Industry, once one of the country's best-known reform schools, whose wards included country singer Merle Haggard, actors Lee J. Cobb and Rory Calhoun, and counter-culture icon Neal Cassady.

But behind the tall red-brick walls of this imposing Romanesque Revival edifice, built on a hill in 1894 in Northern California's gold country, swirl dark and disturbing secrets of violence and murder.

Known locally as merely The Castle, the facility had 77 rooms, 43 fireplaces and a tower festooned with gargoyles. Wards got their introduction to life here by having their heads shaved and then being plunged into a bath full of chemicals to kill lice.

Infractions were dealt with swiftly. "Contrary to what they said at the time, the boys were beaten, severely punished," Donnie Page, Preston Cas-

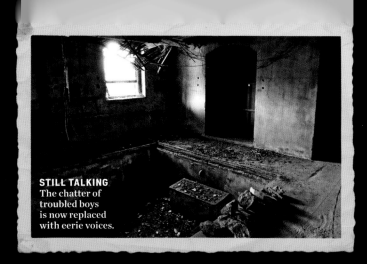

STILL TALKING
The chatter of troubled boys is now replaced with eerie voices.

tle Foundation docent, told the *Sacramento Bee*. "Boys were whipped and thrown in solitary confinement. It was pretty bad."

Several wards died under suspicious circumstances, starting with a 20-year-old convicted burglar who was shot in the back by a guard during an escape attempt in 1919. Ten-dollar bounties were posted on the heads of escapees, and the whole town would join the hunt.

Other wards succumbed to disease or complications from surgical proce-

dures conducted on the cold floors. all, 17 graves of boys populate The C tle's cemetery.

After being shut down in 1960, Castle was abandoned. Fixtures furniture were sold off, and the grou began a slow deterioration, the spi taking the place of the troubled boy

With reports of disembodied voi and doors that slam on their own, wonder Hollywood producers ca here to shoot a 2017 horror mo called *Apparition*.

TEEN SUSPECT
Eugene Monroe (right) faced murder charges.

RETURN VISITOR?
Anna Corbin was bludgeoned to death.

A Brutal Murder

After head housekeeper Anna Corbin was murdered, 657 wards were questioned, but only one was charged: teenager Eugene Monroe, who was never convicted. Some suspected a staff member was the real killer. People say Corbin's ghost still returns to Preston Castle.

"Patients included those who today would not be considered mentally ill."

Doug McCabe, Ohio University

PEACE AND PAIN
For 120 years, the hospital treated thousands of mental patients, but it is best known for lobotomies—and now ghostly sightings.

ATHENS LUNATIC ASYLUM

The truly mad and the tragically misdiagnosed
found their end in anonymous graves.

One day in December, during the brutal winter of 1978, a patient named Margaret Schilling disappeared from the main ward of Ohio's Athens Lunatic Asylum. An intense multi-day search turned up no trace of the 53-year-old, who may have suffered from dementia.

About six weeks later, a maintenance worker found her body behind a locked door in an unused attic. She was lying next to a window, nude, her clothes neatly folded nearby. She had been dead for weeks, likely succumbing to exposure to the intense cold.

But when authorities removed her partially decomposed body, they got a surprise: It left a stain in the outline of a woman on the concrete floor. Efforts to scrub it away failed. To this day, the famed "corpse stain" serves as a ghastly reminder of the disturbing past of what was once one of Ohio's largest mental hospitals, operating from 1874 to 1993.

With patients often admitted for dubious reasons—"masturbation" was cited as a leading cause of insanity in men in the early days—the care seems sadistic by today's standards, including ice water baths, electroshock ther-

apy and lobotomies done with ice picks in eye sockets.

No wonder many claim to see visions of the tortured souls of these suffering patients. Stories place most of the paranormal experiences in the asylum's cemeteries, where nearly 2,000 patients, including 700 women, were buried. About half are identified only by numbers on their headstones.

In 1994, Ohio University took over Athens, renamed it The Ridges and renovated it into offices and classrooms. As for Schilling, the stain remains, and some believe she's still searching for a way out.

BEECHWORTH, AUSTRALIA

BEECHWORTH LUNATIC ASYLUM

Where the mentally ill suffered pain and endured restraints, the most famous ghost is known for her kindness.

HOT SEAT
A chair used for surgical procedures

Strapped into straitjackets, shackled in irons, locked into isolation cages and blasted with electroshock therapy, the damaged souls screamed so loudly they could be heard in the nearby town. Administrators responded by buying a flock of 20 peacocks so the birds' screeches would drown out the noise.

For 128 years, thousands of men and women endured the worst of the Victorian-era treatment at Beechworth. Patients suffered from schizophrenia, severe depression, bipolar disorder, alcoholism and opium addiction. But many others had no business being there at all. With admission requiring only the signatures of two people, Beechworth became a convenient depository for society's inconveniences—quarrelsome teenagers, difficult wives and those unfortunate enough to cross a police officer the wrong way.

Built in 1867 and self-sustaining off the food and livestock from surrounding farmland, Beechworth held 1,200 patients at capacity. An estimated 3,000 patients died there before it closed in 1995. In what is called the most haunted area of the facility, a longtime—and long dead—staff member known as Matron Sharpe, beloved for her kindness to patients, is said to glide down the stairway in her gray hood and period dress. Witnesses say she appears in the dreaded wing where electroshock therapy was carried out, sometimes on many patients at the same time.

Now owned by La Trobe University, much of Beechworth has been converted into a hotel and conference center, with paranormal tours at night.

NO ESCAPE
The admission process made it easy to get a bed—and almost impossible to leave.

Dread Down Under

There is no shortage of Victorian-era scares to be had in Australia. The Aradale Lunatic Asylum (below), a contemporary of Beechworth, reports banging behind the men's isolation cells and mysterious cold gusts from the facility director's office. The imposing Old Geelong Gaol, a maximum-security prison open from 1864 to 1991, has a reputation for mysterious mists and floating orbs. And the Old Melbourne Gaol (1842 to 1929) displays the death masks of executed criminals.

LOUISVILLE, KENTUCKY

WAVERLY HILLS SANATORIUM

Shadows, sounds and a finger down your back welcome you to this crumbling house of death.

IMPOSING EDIFICE
Patients traveled up for care—and often came down dead.

They arrived with burning lungs and fading hopes, only to endure their final days in pain, loneliness—and sometimes madness. They left through a secret tunnel, many forever forgotten.

Today, the disease tuberculosis is treatable with antibiotics. But in the 19th and early 20th centuries, the "White Plague" terrorized America, the highly contagious affliction wiping out entire families. Beginning in 1926, patients came to a five-story gothic monument to suffering known as the Waverly Hills Sanatorium. There was no known cure, and thousands died in agony.

Shuttered decades ago, Waverly fell into disrepair, left to vandals, the elements and, some say, the ghosts. Shadows were said to dance across the graffiti-covered walls, shapeless forms dashing in and out of doorways, crying for help. Lights flickered in rooms abandoned decades ago. The ransacked cafeteria smelled of freshly baked bread.

Some visions return regularly, like the shadow who resembles a man in a doctor's smock and a little girl with a face but no eyes. Shuttered in the 1980s, Waverly was purchased in 2001 by paranormal enthusiasts who have restored it as a historical site for visitors to tour.

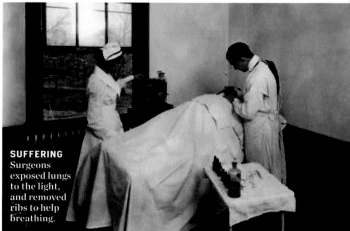

SUFFERING
Surgeons exposed lungs to the light, and removed ribs to help breathing.

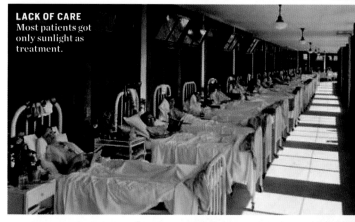

LACK OF CARE
Most patients got only sunlight as treatment.

LONELINESS
Patients rarely received visitors and often died in severe agony.

PAINFUL PAST
The spirits are said to include an overworked doctor in his gown and a depressed nurse who hanged herself.

Death Chute

At the bottom of a steep hill, a rusty, cobweb-covered grate covers what once was the exit portal from the "body chute," a 500-foot tunnel that runs nearly straight down from the sanatorium's main entrance to the railroad tracks. Motorized cables lowered the corpses of TB victims to trains bound for the cemetery or crematorium. Nobody knows how many people made their final journey through the tunnel, its existence hidden from other patients to keep them from panicking. But visitors believe some of the dead lurk there to this day, with reports of sounds and blasts of air—and an unmistakable feeling of not being alone.

BEELITZ-HEILSTATTEN HOSPITAL

The hospital for Adolf Hitler and East German politician Erich Honecker is as creepy as its history.

A sprawling complex of 60 hospital buildings, this facility treated tuberculosis patients from its opening in 1898 until World War I, when the 1,500 beds were filled with casualties from the front. Among the 12,500 soldiers from the German Imperial Army treated by the Red Cross was a young Adolf Hitler, who was wounded in the leg and blinded by mustard gas during the Battle of the Somme against the British and French, earning him the Iron Cross.

The facility treated lung-disease patients again after the war, but its links to Hitler resumed during World War II, when it served as a field hospital for the German leader's Nazi troops. After the Russian Red Army occupied Beelitz-Heilstätten, the hospital treated Russian troops and then Soviet patients for the next 50 years. These included disgraced Communist officials, among them the notorious Erich Honecker after his 1989 ouster as the East German head, before the Berlin Wall fell. Honecker, who had been to the hospital as a German prisoner in WWII, was treated for liver cancer—his condition spared him trial for human rights abuses—before dying in exile.

As the Cold War ended and Germany reunified, most of the grounds were abandoned in the 1990s, including the surgery center, the psychiatric ward and the gun range. For years, the decaying complex served as a ruinous reminder of both the Nazi and Soviet eras, with its haunting history making it a favorite destination for history buffs, urban explorers and movie directors. The grounds were used as locations for Roman Polanski's *The Pianist* in 2002, and *Valkyrie*, starring Tom Cruise, in 2008. To accommodate a growing number of visitors, a 70-foot-tall, 700-foot-long canopied viewing platform named Baum und Zeit, German for tree and time, was constructed in 2015.

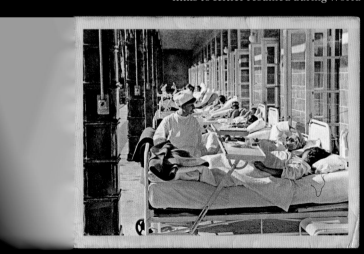

NATURAL REMEDIES
Before antibiotics, tuberculosis patients took "air baths" on a

HAUNTED MEMORIES
"Beelitz particularly retained a real haunting chill even at the height of summer. I suppose it has held some of its darker past in the walls," says Eve Stewart, set designer for *A Cure for Wellness*, a 2016 horror film shot at the hospital.

Touch of Evil

Between 1989 and 1991, a serial killer dubbed the Beast of Beelitz terrorized the city. Wolfgang Schmidt killed six people, including a mom and baby who were walking through the woods near the hospital, where her husband worked.

WASHINGTON, D.C.

ST. ELIZABETHS HOSPITAL

This crumbling psychiatric institution that treated a presidential assassin is on the critical list.

O ne of the first psychiatric hospitals in the United States, the Government Hospital for the Insane (as it was known when it opened in 1855) would take the less-ominous name of St. Elizabeths, but the activities within its walls were still sinister.

In the 1940s, the Office of Strategic Services, the forerunner to the CIA, conducted top-secret truth serum experiments at the Washington, D.C., hospital, plying subjects with mescaline and marijuana to see if the drugs could be used to get Nazi prisoners to talk. The subjects mostly giggled. Later, the hospital conducted lobotomies and electroshock therapy, as well as more than

CRITICAL CONDITION
The National Trust for Historic Preservation named the hospital to its 11 Most Endangered Places list in 2002.

15,000 autopsies, with over 1,400 brains pickled in formaldehyde.

Among the approximately 125,000 patients treated over the decades were Charles J. Guiteau, who assassinated President James Garfield, and would-be assassins Richard Lawrence (who tried to

kill Andrew Jackson) and John Hinckley Jr., who shot Ronald Reagan. Poet Ezra Pound spent 13 years in St. Elizabeths on a treason charge, even though he was sane. After years of decline, the hospital transferred most of its patients to other facilities by the early 2000s.

RUTHIN, WALES

POOL PARK ASYLUM

A former convalescent home is one of the most haunted places in Wales.

Once a deer park for Ruthin Castle in the 1800s, this estate with a mock Tudor-style manor house went through a series of rich owners before it was sold in 1937 to the North Wales Counties Mental Hospital. Taking patients from the Denbigh Insane Asylum, Pool Park (spelled Pool Parc in Welsh) cared for as many as 120 people at a time at its peak of operation.

Closed in 1989, the stately house has never been officially abandoned, but it has fallen into disrepair—the plaster walls peeling, water oozing from the ceilings, windows broken. Reports of strange noises and darting shadows inside the eerie home have attracted ghost hunters,

much to the annoyance of owners trying to renovate the historic building.

Ghost hunter Jason Griffiths of The Ouija Brothers paranormal investigators told Wales Online that he saw a friend being attacked by an aggressive spirit during their visit to the estate, which was also a prisoner of war camp in World War II.

"There's a very dark, heavy presence at Pool Park and if you don't listen to it and pay it attention, it makes itself known," he said. "You can feel when he's near; the surrounding energy becomes heavy."

Another sleuth claimed to have heard a little girl's voice saying, "There's a bad man over there."

THE TERROR ENDS
With no new patients in a decade, the buildings have fallen into decay.

MILLEDGEVILLE, GEORGIA

CENTRAL STATE HOSPITAL

A terrifying trip to this mental facility could land you in an anonymous grave.

Generations of Georgia parents used this threat to get their children to behave: "I'll send you to Milledgeville."

Nothing instilled more fear in a person than the prospect of being dragged to this circa-1892 facility originally called the Georgia Lunatic Asylum, and later Central State Hospital. The facility became the depository of the mentally ill, epileptic and simply strange—all desperate for care but often subjected to abuse and overcrowding.

Patients were plunged into icy showers, strapped into straitjackets, locked in cages, flushed with douches and plied with "nauseants." Doctors would stick lobotomy needles into their brains and zap them with electroshock therapy.

As the patient population grew, the facility expanded to 200 buildings over 2,000 acres. At its peak, a staggering 13,000 people were committed to the asylum, with an abominable patient-to-staff ratio of 100 to 1.

But some patients had no business being there at all. Stories are told of relatives sending insolent teenagers and lovers who dared to date somebody of another race off to Milledgeville. Often, they never left. There are 25,000 patients buried on the facility's grounds, 2,000 of them identified by numbers instead of names on cast-iron markers.

In 1959, a Pulitzer Prize–winning investigation by the *Atlanta Constitution* found that conditions were even worse than many people thought, with some

so-called doctors recruited from among the population. The patients were literally running the asylum.

The combination of reforms and advances in psychiatric medication gradually reduced Milledgeville's numbers until the facility accepted its last patient in 2010. Now, only a handful remain at a dramatically downsized facility.

Some buildings became prisons; the rest were abandoned. According to Dr. Mab Segrest, a professor researching the facility's history for a book, "Many of the stories haven't really been told publicly because they are hard to talk about, and there's a lot of shame tied to the history surrounding Central State Hospital."

"It has witnessed the heights of man's humanity and the depths of his degradation."
Ex-staffer Dr. Peter G. Cranford

DOWN THE DRAIN
Once the largest mental hospital in the world, it now holds only memories of abuse and neglect.

Central State Hospital
Annual Report
July 1, 1984 - June 30, 1985

Central State Hospital
Annua
July 1,

THIELLS, NEW YORK

LETCHWORTH VILLAGE

Patients endured severe abuse before this hellhole was shut down.

It was to be a sanctuary for the "feeble-minded," a quiet community to provide a humane setting for those suffering from mental illnesses who normally would have been locked in asylums or prison cells.

Opened in 1911, Letchworth Village spread over 2,300 rural acres an hour north of Manhattan, with tidy quarters for dozens of patients.

The first residents ranged from children to the elderly, living communally and self-sufficiently. They grew their own crops and tended to chickens and cows. They made toys to raise money.

And it was here, in 1950, that the first trials of a vaccine for the then-scourge of polio were administered to 20 children. It was considered a success, with 17 children developing antibodies and none suffering complications.

But the doors of the neoclassic dormitories and dining halls hid a village of secrets. As the population soared to 4,000 in the 1950s and funding fell short, the residents crowded into hallways and day rooms, sleeping on mattresses thrown on the floor.

They were poorly clothed and suffered malnutrition from a lack of food. They were neglected by a staff stretched thin. Some were beaten and raped.

Then there were the stories of macabre medical practices, of harvested brains floating in jars of formaldehyde. Even the polio trials had a dark side: Those children were unable to give consent and had no choice but to become guinea pigs.

In 1972, Geraldo Rivera blew the lid off Letchworth Village and a similar institution in Staten Island, New York, in a documentary called *Willowbrook: The Last Great Disgrace* that showed moaning children lying naked in feces, among other horrors. "Inside we have housed the children of many of our citizens who are subjected to what appears to be the worst possible conditions I've ever seen in my life," noted Bronx congressman Mario Biaggi in the documentary.

Shuttered in 1996, Letchworth Village is now an eerie, empty city of decay and painful memories, memorialized by the plots in the old cemetery with hundreds of T-shaped markers but no names.

CAVED IN
Shuttered after 85 years, the buildings crumbled.

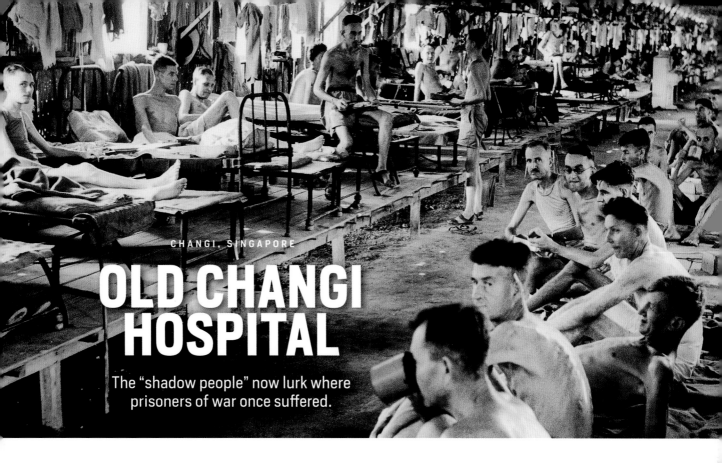

OLD CHANGI HOSPITAL

The "shadow people" now lurk where prisoners of war once suffered.

Wander through the Old Changi Hospital at your own risk. Stories tell of visitors veering off from group tours with another person and finding themselves in a lonely part of this hospital/prison camp. There, somebody who looks like one of your friends will issue a warning that you don't belong here—then disappear.

These accounts, staples in the paranormal blog Hungzai: Singapore's Freakiest Online Ghost Stories, add to the eerie reputation of this nearly century-old, creepy, crumbling facility in Singapore, a former military hospital seized by the Japanese during World War II.

It operated again as a hospital for decades after the war, but the complex was abandoned in 1997, leaving it to "shadow people" and the ghosts of former patients and inmates rumored to have been tortured by the Japanese secret police.

So chilling is this setting that producers shot the found-footage horror movie *Haunted Changi* on location at Old Changi, only to find that the scares continued even when the cameras stopped shooting, with the crew and actors recalling caresses from unseen hands, and visions of a floating woman.

As scary as the ghost stories are, they don't hold a candle to real-life history. A plaque outside the hospital marks the site where 66 Chinese civilian men who opposed Japanese occupation were bound together with ropes and mowed down by machine-gun firing squads.

REAL HORRORS The cast and crew of a 2010 fright flick got more than they bargained for.

TRANS-ALLEGHENY

The abandoned wards of this "lunatic asylum" echo with patients' anguished cries.

The original idea was to make life better for the mentally stricken: Build a modern facility with staggered wings to bring in sunlight and fresh air, and staff it with doctors and nurses trained in the latest treatments.

Prison laborers and Irish immigrant stonemasons constructed the Trans-Allegheny Lunatic Asylum from 1858 to 1881 (with an interruption for the Civil War), and it seemed to fulfill its early promise. An impressive four-story structure with a 200-foot clock tower and 921 windows, it offered what was state-of-the-art care in a self-sufficient setting, operating its own farm, dairy, gas well, waterworks and cemetery over 666 acres.

But despite the best of intentions, life for patients was far from ideal behind the 2-foot-thick walls. Many were admitted for dubious reasons: "female disease," "political excitement," "novel reading." The facility was often a dumping ground for society's unwanted and difficult, the drug addicts, epileptics and uppity wives.

As the years wore on, things grew worse. Designed to house 250 patients, the asylum swelled to a population of 2,400 by the 1950s, and the facility couldn't keep up. The sanitation was poor, the lighting dim and the temperatures cold in the West Virginia winters.

Patients who couldn't be controlled by staff or drugs found themselves locked in cages. Violence erupted in the crowded wards, with reports of female workers getting raped by patients.

One woman simply disappeared, her body found two months later at the end of an abandoned staircase.

When a new facility was built in 1994, officials shut down Trans-Allegheny and left it there to rot. Walls crumbled, paint peeled, graffiti scarred the grounds. What the elements and vandals didn't destroy, city employees found playing paintball in the halls did.

In 2007, the facility sold at auction for the bargain-basement price of $1.5 million to private investors, and today only the ghosts of the patients who never knew they were supposed to leave occupy the wards.

Trans-Allegheny is now a paranormal playground, filled with the mysterious rattlings of old gurneys and disembodied moanings of patients who had lobotomies performed with an ice pick–like instrument. Dark visions dart behind rusted doors.

Brave guests can take nighttime tours, though *The Washington Post*'s Kathy Legg notes, "You really would have to be out of your mind to spend a night in this building."

VIOLENT END
Overcrowding and patient abuse doomed this once-model facility.

DECAYING SCHOOLS AND ORPHANAGES

Facilities meant to teach and shelter hold only ghostly memories.

MILLBROOK, NEW YORK
HALCYON HALL

A luxury hotel that went bust, the five-story, 200-room Halcyon Hall in the village of Millbrook, New York, was sold out of bankruptcy in 1907 and used as an expansion for the Bennett School for Girls. Here, the daughters of rich families studied amid opulence: tennis courts, a putting green, horse stables and an outdoor theater. Renamed Bennett College when the school became a junior college for women, enrollment declined in the 1970s, as single-gender colleges fell out of favor. Renovations and upgrades strained the college's finances, and in 1977 Bennett was again bankrupt, this time closing for good.

The school suffered water damage from burst pipes and looters cleaned out anything of value left behind. Seized by banking regulators in 1991, today the Queen Anne–style structure built in 1893 resembles a sagging, creepy haunted house as preservationists fight to save it.

CHERTSEY, ENGLAND
SILVERLANDS ORPHANAGE

A glamorous 19th-century estate with dazzling chandeliers, mahogany paneling, a grand staircase and a dramatic neo-Georgian lobby became a home for destitute children in 1938 when the house was taken over by The Actors' Orphanage. The facility weathered World War II—the children were evacuated to New York during the conflict—but couldn't survive the staggering costs of maintenance and repairs. In 1958, it was shuttered and the building left empty for decades. A plan in the 1990s to house sex offenders was scuttled after years of fierce opposition from local residents, who held candlelight vigils to protest. The property has since fallen further into decay.

ST. LOUIS, MISSOURI
CARR SCHOOL

Designed by noted architect William B. Ittner, the Carr School educated generations of children after opening in 1908. The handsome building included colorful touches, like mosaics of children, and the kindergarten area was state-of-the-art. But after closing in 1983, the school grounds fell prey to vandals and weeds, and its owners have been unable to raise the funds for renovation. Extensive damage from a fire in 2018 placed the site's future into further doubt.

ISTANBUL, TURKEY
PRINKIPO ORPHANAGE

Built at the end of the 19th century as a massive timber casino, the Prinkipo Palace on Büyükada island off Istanbul never saw a single bet placed. The project was abandoned when the religious—and fiercely anti-gambling—34th sultan of the Ottoman Empire objected.

In 1903, a rich Greek banker's wife bought the ornate structure, and donated it to the Eastern Orthodox Church, which converted it into an orphanage. After five-plus decades, the Prinkipo Greek Orthodox Orphanage closed due to political strife between Turkey and Greece. The vacant property was seized by Turkey in 1997, then returned to Greece. But damage by fire and rot means it may not survive.

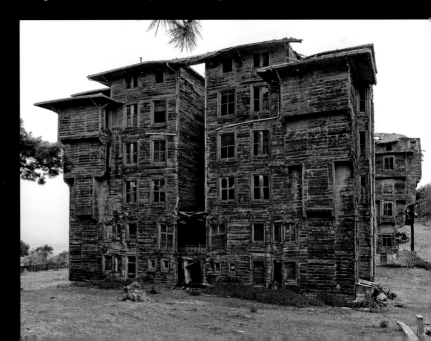

HAUNTED HOUSES

IN THESE SCENES OF
VIOLENT CRIMES OF
PASSION AND REVENGE,
THE WALLS DON'T JUST
SPEAK—THEY SCREAM.

FALL RIVER, MASSACHUSETTS

LIZZIE BORDEN HOUSE

Good luck getting 40 winks at the scene of 40 whacks in this bloody B&B.

A once-popular children's jump-rope rhyme goes like this: "Lizzie Borden took an ax and gave her mother forty whacks. When she saw what she had done, she gave her father forty-one."

Just a little ditty to play over in your mind if you're thinking of spending the night in a neat, two-story clapboard Victorian house that also happened to be the scene of one of the most notorious crimes of all time.

The ax murders of 32-year-old Lizzie Borden's father and stepmother one steamy August morning in 1892, and the case's shocking conclusion, have resonated through history. Despite acting strangely (she was spotted burning her own dress) and giving conflicting stories, Lizzie was acquitted of the murders and lived out her life in Fall River, Massachusetts, although she was ostracized.

The home has since been restored to its homicidal glory as the Lizzie Borden Bed & Breakfast Museum. Visitors can see the exact spot where Andrew Borden's body was found on a sofa. The more adventurous can sleep in the room where Abby Borden's body was found in a pool of blood on the floor.

And no night would be complete without creaking floors, squeaky doors opening and closing, disembodied voices, the feel of a finger down the back and the vision of Lizzie's ghost in the basement, where she allegedly stashed evidence.

WALKED FREE
Lizzie Borden was never convicted of the infamous ax murders.

DEAD STEPMOM
Abby Borden was murdered while making a bed.

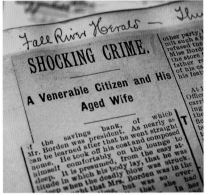

SHOCKING CRIME.

A Venerable Citizen and His Aged Wife

HATCHET JOB
Andrew Borden may have been sleeping when he was killed.

MODEST HOME
Although wealthy, the Bordens lived frugally.

LOS ANGELES, CALIFORNIA

MANSON HOUSE

The cult leader's "family" unleashed a bloody massacre
at a celebrity home in the Hollywood Hills.

For much of its history, the 1941-built home with a pool and guest house in Benedict Canyon, above Bel Air, symbolized Hollywood glamour. Its residents had included newly married Cary Grant and Dyan Cannon, Henry Fonda, and the '60s pop group Paul Revere & the Raiders. Record producer Terry Melcher (Doris Day's son) rented the house around the time he was discussing a record and documentary deal with a fledgling musician named Charles Manson.

Melcher ultimately decided not to move forward with the project, and Manson never forgave him. On the night of August 8, 1969, four members of the cult leader's "family" invaded the French-style country house at 10050 Cielo Drive and slaughtered five people. Melcher and his then-girlfriend Candice Bergen were not among them, having moved out for new tenants: actress Sharon Tate and her husband, director Roman Polanski.

Whether Manson knew of the change in residency remains a burning question, but he knew the house; he'd been there at least twice. Either way, his followers did what they were told to do—murder everybody there, including Tate, eight months pregnant (Polanski was in Europe for a film).

For the next 20 years, landlord Rudi Altobelli lived there—saying he felt "safe"—before selling it in 1989 for $1.6 million. Nine Inch Nails rocker Trent Reznor then rented the home and set up a recording studio he called "Le Pig" after the word Susan Atkins had scrawled in Tate's blood on the front door.

"Little sounds would make me jump at first, but after a while it was just like home," he told *Entertainment Weekly*. "The house didn't feel terrifying so much as sad—peacefully sad."

The structure was razed in 1994 and rebuilt with a new address. But next-door neighbor David Oman says the evil remains, telling *LA Weekly* he awoke one night to find a "full body apparition" by his bed. The ghost, he says, was pointing toward the former 10050 Cielo Drive.

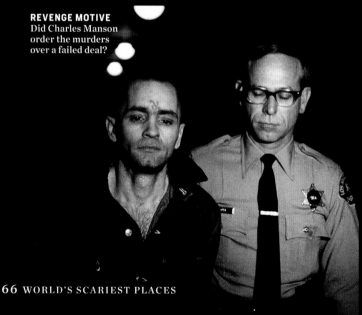

REVENGE MOTIVE
Did Charles Manson
order the murders
over a failed deal?

GRIM REPUTATION
Before the murders,
the house drew
celebrity tenants.

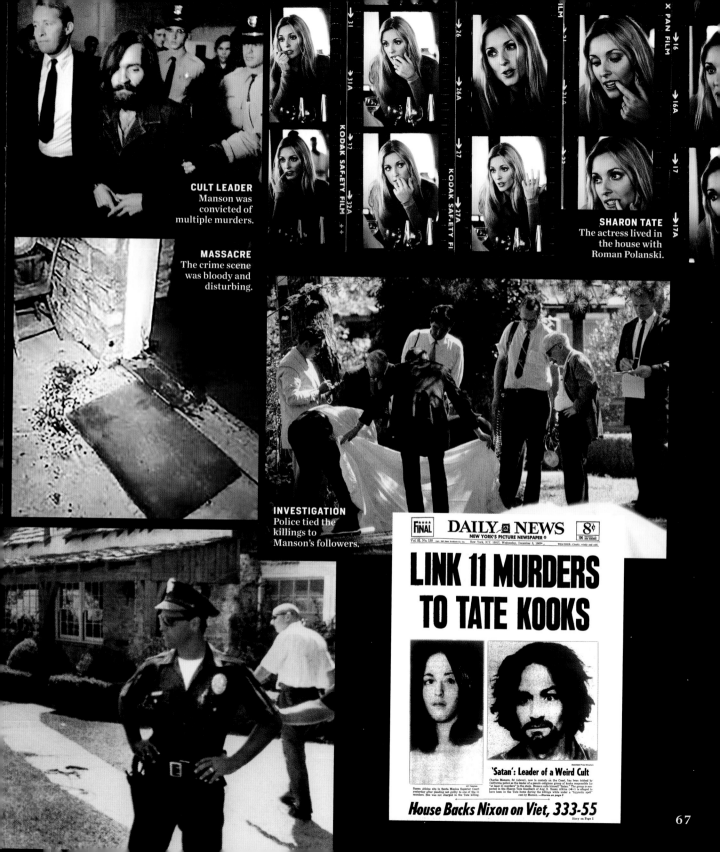

CULT LEADER
Manson was
convicted of
multiple murders.

SHARON TATE
The actress lived in
the house with
Roman Polanski.

MASSACRE
The crime scene
was bloody and
disturbing.

INVESTIGATION
Police tied the
killings to
Manson's followers.

FINAL ★★★★ **DAILY NEWS** 8¢
NEW YORK'S PICTURE NEWSPAPER ®
Vol. 51, No. 138   New York, N.Y. 10017, Wednesday, December 3, 1969   WEATHER: Cloudy, windy and cold.

LINK 11 MURDERS
TO TATE KOOKS

'Satan': Leader of a Weird Cult

Charles Manson, 34 (above), now in custody on the Coast, has been tabbed by
California police as the leader of a pseudo-religious group of kooks responsible for
"at least 11 murders" in the state. Manson calls himself "Satan." The group is suspected in the Sharon Tate bloodbath of Aug. 9. Susan Atkins (◄—) is alleged to
have been in the Tate home during the killings while under a "hypnotic spell"
cast by Manson.—Stories on page 3

*Susan Atkins sits in Santa Monica Superior Court
yesterday after pleading not guilty to one of the 11
murders. She was not charged in the Tate killing.*

House Backs Nixon on Viet, 333-55
Story on Page 5

67

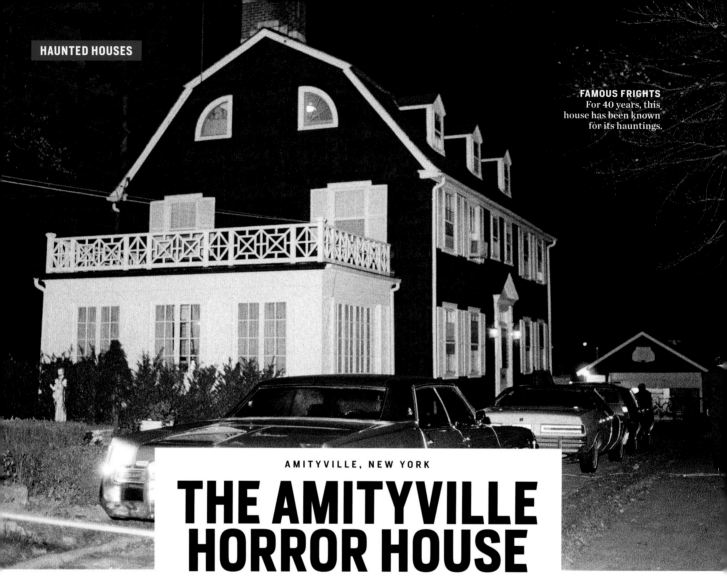

FAMOUS FRIGHTS
For 40 years, this
house has been known
for its hauntings.

AMITYVILLE, NEW YORK

THE AMITYVILLE HORROR HOUSE

The world's most famous haunted house spawned books, movies—and skepticism.

In 1974, Ronald "Butch" DeFeo, 23, killed his parents and four siblings with a rifle in their home in the Amityville neighborhood of Long Island, New York, a horrific crime for which DeFeo got six life sentences.

Despite the house's well-publicized history, the Lutz family purchased the five-bedroom Dutch Colonial with windows that look like eyes, only to endure what they called 28 days of pure madness: green slime oozing from the walls; a wall-mounted crucifix that swung upside down and started stinking; a pig that somehow climbed to an upstairs window.

George and Kathy Lutz fled with their family, then hooked up with author Jay Anson—a collaboration that produced the terrifying 1977 best-seller *The Amity-ville Horror: A True Story* and the 1979 film by the same name, starring James Brolin and Margot Kidder as the Lutzes.

This spawned a mini empire of some 13 more films along with TV specials, documentaries and books. It also raised one big question: Is the world's most famous haunted house really haunted?

The October 2018 release *The Amity-ville Murders* explores the psychosis of

MURDEROUS MYSTERY
Why Butch DeFeo slaughtered his family remains unknown.

DeFeo—who says he was urged on to kill by voices he heard inside the house. But many of the previous movies have almost nothing to do with the original demonic doings, save for the name "Amityville" in the titles. And almost from the moment the first book hit the shelves, controversy swirled over how true that story was. Lawsuits also erupted over the proceeds from the Amityville projects. The Lutzes reportedly agreed to split the book profits with Anson, but attorney William E. Weber, who defended DeFeo, also wanted a piece of the action, claiming the couple once had a deal with him and a different writer. He claimed the whole Amityville story was pure fiction. "I know this book's a hoax," Weber told *People* magazine in 1979. "We created this horror story over many bottles of wine."

It seems the only thing haunting this house was litigation.

How to Sell a Haunted House

You'd think a mass murder followed by demonic pigs and slimy walls would dent a home's curb appeal. Not so. The Amityville Horror House has sold several times over the years, and your haunted house can, too. Realtors label a property like this "stigmatized" by an event, real or rumored, that could hurt the asking price despite the lack of any physical damage. This includes houses with suicides, murders and sometimes spirits. State laws differ over whether ghostly goings-on amount to a "material fact" that must be disclosed to potential buyers. While many laws are governed by the principle of caveat emptor, or "buyer beware," many realtors come down on the side of caution and reveal the haunted history. That's because nothing is scarier than a lawsuit.

VILLISCA, IOWA

VILLISCA AX MURDER HOUSE

For more than a century, the unsolved killings of six children and two adults have haunted a town.

Sometime between midnight and 5 a.m. on June 10, 1912, in a white frame house in southwestern Iowa, a family of six and two others were bludgeoned to death in their beds with an ax. They were killed with such ferocity that the weapon left dents in the ceiling from the upswing.

The brutal slaying of Josiah and Sarah Moore, their four children, and the two 5-year-old Stillinger sisters baffled police. In the era before the careful sealing of crime scenes and the widespread use of fingerprint and other forensic evidence, the few clues left behind—the wiped-clean ax, a watch chain that apparently belonged to the killer—proved of little use.

Several suspects were identified, including a traveling preacher, a prominent state senator and a killer hired by a business rival of Josiah's. But none was charged with the crime, and after more than 100 years, the Villisca Ax Murders case is officially still open.

The violence continues to haunt the small town—to say nothing of the house where it happened. Tours and overnight

stays are available, but be forewarned: Visitors report the sounds of children playing when no kids are in the house. There have been accounts of ladders that move on their own and lamps that fall for no apparent reason. A parade of psychics and paranormal investigators claim to have made contact with otherworldly beings there. Will the victims not rest until their killings are solved?

THE INNOCENT Of the eight ax-murder victims, six were children.

The Story of Villisca's Unparalleled Tragedy, as Told on This and Succeeding Pages. The Review, Thursday Morning, June 13. Latest Developments

THE VILLISCA RE[VIEW]

VOL. XLI. NO. 46   VILLISCA, IOWA, THURSDAY, JUNE 13, 1912

8 PEOPLE MURDERED IN THEIR BEDS IN VILLISC[A]

Family of J. B. Moore, Numbering Six, and Two Daughters of Mr. and Mrs. J. T. Stillinger the Victims

MOTIVE FOR CRIME LACKING

Heads of All Crushed With Ax, and Murderer Escapes Leaving No Clue—Crime Is Unparalleled In History of State

J. B. MOORE, age 43   MRS. J. B. MOORE, age 39

THE DEAD:
J. B. Moore, age 43
Mrs. Moore, age 39

RESTLESS SPIRITS
Will solving the crime quiet the ghosts?

SAMUT SAKHON, THAILAND

MURDER MANSION

A family's senseless slaughter turns a Thai home into a crime time-capsule.

Once a showcase multi-story home with a dramatic skylight, this mansion in the Bangkok suburb of Samut Sakhon sits eerily deserted, a magnet for snakes, lizards, drug addicts and vandals.

Somebody scrawled haunting messages in red paint on a peeling wall—and indeed, reminders of the horrors that visited this house can't be ignored. According to local lore, a family of three was murdered in the mansion sometime after they moved there in the 1970s.

Photographer Dax Ward, who documented the chilling residence, says his research showed that the Chinese-Thai victims—a mother, father and child—

SIGNS OF TROUBLE
Messages written on the walls recall
the horrors experienced within.

were recent arrivals whose thriving business drew the attention of robbers, who broke into the house one night.

"The burglary seems to have got out of hand and the criminals murdered the entire family and took whatever cash and valuables they could," Ward said in 2019. "They got away, and as far as anyone knows, they've never been caught."

The cursed house remains frozen in time, with the kitchen plates, furniture, a bed, lamps and shoes left in place. Ward said that his visit was "certainly eerie" as he walked through the dilapidated home, which has been damaged by fires.

"There was an old, rusty knife lying on the upper floor, which I found to be a bit creepy," he added. "It is awful to imagine the horrific crime that was committed there."

SEGUIN LIGHTHOUSE

Isolation, madness and murder hang over this historic beacon on a lonely island.

The Seguin Island lighthouse invites awe: It's a soaring 180-foot tower with a powerful beam guiding ships through the treacherous rocks off the coast of Maine. But for one young bride, this was a place of pure misery.

According to lore, in the 1850s, a recently married lighthouse keeper brought his wife to Seguin Island, but the isolation and loneliness plunged her into a deep depression.

To lift his bride's spirits and battle her boredom, the keeper had a piano shipped to the tiny island, 2 miles offshore. To his initial joy, she played. And then she never stopped.

Day after day, night after night she played the same song, either because that was the only sheet music she had, or because she was going mad—the stories differ—driving her husband batty until one day he snapped.

He took an ax to the piano, and then to his wife, and then to himself.

Though never verified, the story casts a long shadow over the historic lighthouse, commissioned in 1795, rebuilt a couple of times and staffed by the Coast Guard until 1985, at which time its light and foghorn were automated.

Though nobody lives here anymore, it is said the lighthouse is hardly empty. Captains report the sounds of a piano wafting through the fog from the direction of the island, and some visitors say they believe they've seen the ghost of a man lofting an ax above his head.

DO YOU HEAR IT?
Captains say this lighthouse emits piano music from a lonely spirit.

BRAN, ROMANIA

BRAN CASTLE

Dracula's castle may exist only in books, so sink your teeth into the next best, and scariest, thing.

GOTHIC HORROR
The 15th-century fortress towers over the dark forest.

STAIRWAY TO HELL
Dimly lit halls and secret passageways give off castle creeps.

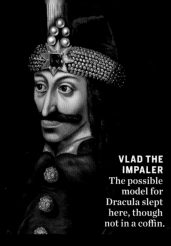

VLAD THE IMPALER
The possible model for Dracula slept here, though not in a coffin.

I n the horror classic *Dracula*, the castle inhabited by a blood-sucking count sits on "the very edge of a terrific precipice" above a chasm where the rivers "wind in deep gorges through the forests" of Transylvania.

As the only castle in Transylvania even vaguely fitting that description, Bran Castle in modern-day Romania attracts hundreds of thousands of tourists a year wanting to sink their teeth into the chilling Dracula story.

Built in the 14th century on a cliff on the strategically important Bran Pass, Bran Castle places visitors in an elaborate medieval world with secret passageways, tunneled stone staircases, conical towers and antique-filled rooms.

At night, the wind whips through the dense forest below, the bearskin-covered floors creek and the walls shudder, and it's easy to imagine the days when the castle served as a stopover for Vlad the Impaler, a hero to many Romanians and Bulgarians as a warrior knight who had an unsavory killing style.

Just how connected Bran Castle is to Dracula's castle invites debate. The book's edifice—like its menacing lord—comes from the imagination of Irish writer Bram Stoker, who never traveled to Transylvania and never visited Bran Castle, though there's speculation Stoker may have seen illustrations of it in an 1860s book about Transylvania, and that Count Dracula could have

been based in part on Vlad the Impaler.

Scholars scoff at the comparisons, saying *Dracula*'s crumbling castle bears little resemblance to tidy Bran Castle and that its location was probably inspired by a bare hilltop in the Alps. No matter how tenuous the links may be, visitors insist Bran Castle certainly has the feel of Dracula's haunts, so welcoming to children of the night.

"You could feel the evil in the walls. You knew that you weren't alone," Canadian Tami Varma told CBC News after winning a contest to spend a Halloween night in the castle. "We may have been the only physical guests there, but there were certainly invisible guests amongst us."

"The wind was blasting at the windows all night. It was snowing. It was like out of a nightmare."

Tami Varma to the *Ottawa Citizen* about her castle overnighter

Drac's Digs?
Two other Romanian castles have been linked to the Count. The 15th-century moat-ringed Corvin Castle (left) supposedly held Vlad as prisoner, and the 13th-century Poenari Castle appeared in a Starz TV episode of *Da Vinci's Demons* about the Impaler. But researchers say Bram Stoker had never heard of either castle.

FORBIDDEN WATERS Voices and visions are reported in the pool area.

LONG BEACH, CALIFORNIA
QUEEN MARY

The venerable ocean liner is crowned the world's most haunted ship.

How an 18-year-old firefighter known as "Half Hatch Harry" came to be crushed by a heavy door in the engine room remains one of the many mysteries of the *Queen Mary,* the stately ship that carried troops, war brides and celebrities from Hollywood's golden age in speed and style.

These doors, deep in the bowels of the ship, take a full 60 seconds to shut completely. It could well be that poor Harry was as confused as anybody else about his demise in 1966, which may explain why he's still spotted hanging around below: He's seeking answers.

The 1,000-foot-long liner sailed the Atlantic from 1936 until 1967, when she was permanently docked as a tourist attraction in Long Beach's harbor. The passengers are said to be replaced by some 150 ghosts, making this lady of the seas the world's most haunted vessel.

Bathing beauties in vintage 1930s swimsuits materialize around the first-class swimming pool. Little girls who supposedly drowned in the second-class pool have been seen playing together. One older fellow has been spotted wandering the Main Deck.

The ship's operators have decided to capitalize on public interest in the eerie activity and offer organized nightly tours through the ship's bowels for guests who want to explore the paranormal, and hold an annual "Dark Harbor" onboard haunted Halloween party.

But the scariest place on the ship may be stateroom 340 in what is now a hotel, with reports of a toilet that flushes

MARITIME MARVEL Bigger and faster than the *Titanic,* the *Queen Mary* crossed the Atlantic 1,001 times.

on its own, flying bedsheets and the terrifying presence of a man warning to "Get out!" Guests complained so much that the stateroom was once closed to visitors and the room numbers removed. Today, if you dare, you can choose to stay overnight in the "ghost suite." The nightly rate includes a chest with a Ouija board for private seances, a crystal ball, tarot cards and ghost-hunting equipment.

FRIGHT HOUSE
Spirits of presidents and their wives are said to roam the executive mansion.

THE WHITE HOUSE

Hail to the chief ghosts! Presidential spirits haunt 1600 Pennsylvania Avenue.

The story goes that British Prime Minister Winston Churchill, visiting in the White House, emerged from a long bath only to confront the ghost of Abraham Lincoln. Churchill happened to be stark naked at the time—but in full possession of his wits. "Good evening, Mr. President," he said. "You seem to have me at a disadvantage." Lincoln just smiled and vanished.

Only Churchill—and, perhaps, Lincoln—knows if this famous tale is true. Still, it stands as one of many 1600 Pennsylvania Avenue stories. The spirit of Lincoln has also been felt by the wives of presidents Calvin Coolidge, Theodore Roosevelt and

ANDREW JACKSON
Old Hickory's laughter and cursing echo through the White House.

Lyndon Johnson, as well as the queen of the Netherlands, who saw him in his top hat—and promptly fainted.

Abe is not the only spirit roaming about. Abigail Adams, wife of second president John Adams, has been reputed to move about in a cap and shawl, sometimes appearing as if she's carrying laundry. President William Howard Taft supposedly saw her floating through doors. James Madison's wife, Dolley, is said to show up in the Rose Garden, which she originally planted in the early 1800s, and her spirit once chided gardeners not to dig it up. Thomas Jefferson has been heard playing his violin, William Henry Harrison stomps through the attic, and John Tyler keeps proposing over and over to his wife. And a potty-mouthed Andrew Jackson is said to make repeat appearances.

77

CHÂTEAU MIRANDA

A magical castle out of a Disney film crumbles into ruins after the doors shut and nobody comes to the rescue.

Château Miranda went from something out of a fairy tale to the setting of a horror movie.

Built in the 19th century originally for French aristocrats who were fleeing angry commoners—and the guillotine—during the French Revolution, the castle dazzled in the Belgian province of Namur, southeast of Brussels, with its spires, towering ceilings, more than 500 windows, a clock tower and gardens.

A neo-Gothic marvel from famed English landscape architect Edward Milner, Castle Miranda served as the home of the descendants of the Liedekerke-DeBeaufort family until World War II, when German soldiers occupied the grounds during the Battle of the Bulge.

Belgium's national railway company took over after the war and converted the castle to an orphanage and vacation camp for sick kids, giving the estate its new name, "Château de Noisy."

By 1980, with the orphanage and camp shut down, the din of frolicking children gave way to an eerie silence as the castle was little-used. Maintenance and operating costs mounted, and it was abandoned in 1991, falling prey to vandals and the elements. After a fire

and storm weakened the structure, workers dismantled the conical Gothic roof peaks in 2016.

A search for a new owner has so far failed, and now only urban explorers and ghost hunters roam Château Miranda's decrepit halls, the floors littered with dust and debris and the once-grand staircases collapsing.

There are eerie discoveries to be made within. Amid the crumbling pillars below the peeling ceilings, old dolls are scattered on the floors, and a few, for some unknown reason, hang from the walls. Listen carefully and you can still hear the mechanisms of the century-old clock, even though it hasn't been serviced in decades. (While the clock technically works, it tells the wrong time.)

Château Miranda is now so ominous that Hollywood took notice: It played the role of Castle Lecter in the NBC TV show *Hannibal*.

SPIRES
The neo-Gothic masterpiece is being swallowed up by nature.

CASTLE DESPAIR
The building went from grandeur to rubble after it was abandoned in 1991.

LOCH AWE, SCOTLAND

KILCHURN CASTLE

A late–medieval structure built on a rocky peninsula is said to be haunted by a sobbing child.

This 15th-century, much-photographed castle was built for the Campbells of Glenorchy, members of a powerful clan, on what was formerly an island in Loch Awe, Scotland. The courtyard castle consisted of a five-story rectangular tower with a cellar and prison on the ground floor, a hall on the first floor and bedrooms above.

It was slowly added to over the years; in 1690, after the first Jacobite Rising, it was converted into a garrison capable of housing 200 troops. The tower was converted into officers' quarters.

Seventy years later, a storm badly damaged the structure when a lightning strike blew off one of the turrets, which landed in the courtyard upside down but in one piece. Kilchurn was aban-

doned in the 1700s, but visitors can still see the circular top of the tower lying in the courtyard where it fell.

Some guests have claimed to hear a disembodied voice crying for help during their visits—it is said to be the ghost of a child who was walled up in the upper part of the tower.

CLEAR PATHWAY
In the 1500s, the isolated castle was accessed by a tunnel under the loch. Water levels have since dropped, and the island is now a peninsula.

HOPING FOR GLORY
Piotr Kazimierczak is fighting local plans to demolish his unfinished masterpiece.

ŁAPALICE CASTLE

An artist's ambitious project sits unfinished in a small Polish village.

It was supposed to be a modest residence, but sculptor Piotr Kazimierczak had some bigger ideas. What began in 1979 as a single-family house with a small studio in a tiny Polish village grew into a palace that came to be called Łapalice Castle, with 52 rooms, a swimming pool and a dozen turrets, one for each of Jesus' 12 apostles.

It would have kept growing had Kazimierczak not run out of money and the local authorities not run out of patience as the estate spilled onto land for which he did not have permits. Construction stopped in 1991, with the castle now an unfinished shell attracting vandals—even as the artist clings to hope his grand vision may one day be realized.

SPIRALING AWAY
The castle uses construction techniques from hundreds of years ago.

DARMSTADT, GERMANY

CASTLE FRANKENSTEIN

An old locale in Germany cashes in on tenuous links to Mary Shelley's Gothic novel.

For the local residents, the name of this imposing medieval Gothic edifice in Darmstadt, Germany, would have held no sinister significance. Combining the words "Frank" for a Germanic tribe and "stein" for stone, many places and structures were called Frankenstein. But no other castle had such a dark reputation as Castle Frankenstein.

Inside the forbidding walls of this 13th-century castle, a doctor and alchemist named Johann Konrad Dippel was rumored to have performed experiments on bodies he dug up from graves in the 1700s, stirring fears among the local clergy that he had created a monster by jolting a corpse to life with electricity from lightning.

Whether these tales ever reached a 17-year-old Mary Shelley when she visited a nearby town a century-and-a-half later has never been established. But soon after, she began writing her widely famous 1818 novel, *Frankenstein*, with obvious parallels, and that's enough to draw droves of fans to this crumbling edifice, particularly around Halloween.

IT'S ALIVE! A dragon was believed to live in the garden of the monster's castle.

KIPLIN HALL

This centuries-old estate is equipped with a tunnel of terror.

One of the great estates of England, Kiplin Hall boasts impeccably manicured gardens, four towers, and ornate rooms stuffed with paintings and vintage furniture from the four families who've occupied this grand country house over the past four centuries.

But for the many visitors who come to North Yorkshire for tours, Kiplin Hall offers something much more: a good scare. "There is the history of people and the building, great change, great passion and some very good ghost sto-ries indeed," British historian Lesley Smith says on the TV show *Most Haunted,* which counts Kiplin Hall as one of the scariest places in Britain, if not the world, full of spirits, spooky sounds and unexplained events.

Built by the River Swale in 1619 as a hunting lodge for George Calvert, sec-retary of state to James I and, later, one of the founders of Maryland in what would become the United States, Kiplin Hall grew and changed as it was passed through marriage to different families over the years.

The Gothic drawing room built in the early 1800s was the largest addition, and today it's rife with paranormal activity: cold spots, a doctor looming over a piano, and a little girl in distress. But the creepiest area is said to be a tun-nel built in the 18th century that joins the service wing to the north tower. Once used as a passageway for servants, the tunnel now serves as a path for the undead, with disembodied footsteps echoing off the walls and regular sight-ings of a female specter, forever pacing her eerie aisle.

AUSTERE ABODE
A bland exterior hides a lively history of haunts.

LONDON, ENGLAND

TOWER OF LONDON

Anguished cries and gruesome specters of beheaded royals are said to roam the castle.

Once upon a simple and more brutal time, politics in Britain could be brutally simple: Anger a king, lose a head. Many of those on the losing side of a royal row wound up on the chopping block at the Tower of London. The luckier ones rotted in their cells.

Built on the banks of the Thames by William the Conqueror in 1078 and expanded and modified over the centuries, the Tower has served many purposes, from fortress to palace. These days, it's the official keeper of the Crown Jewels—and the residence of the Crown's ghosts.

King Henry VIII's second wife, Anne Boleyn, who bore him a future queen (Elizabeth I) but not a son—among other insults, real and invented—is said to walk the corridors minus her head, which she lost in 1536 after going on trial for treason.

Visitors also report the anguished sobs of Lady Arbella Stuart, who died in the Tower in 1615. Arrested by King James, who worried that her marriage to William Seymour (who was sixth in line to the throne) threatened James' own reign, Arbella escaped—but was caught and incarcerated in the Tower. Refusing to eat until she saw her husband again, she eventually died of hunger—and a broken heart..

Then there are the spirits of the two princes in the Tower: boys aged 9 and 12 who have been spotted scampering around in their nightshirts. The boys vanished from the Tower in 1483, probably murdered to secure their uncle's hold on the throne. A box containing two small skeletons that could have been theirs was found under the White Tower nearly 200 years later.

Perhaps the most terrifying ghost, though, is that of the Countess of Salisbury, Margaret Pole, who died in 1541 in the worst possible way. Ordered to be executed as an enemy of Henry VIII on the basis of evidence that was probably planted, a defiant Margaret refused to kneel for her beheading. The frustrated executioner chased her around the scaffold and hacked her apart in front of the horrified crowd. Listen for Margaret's screams still echoing through the Tower.

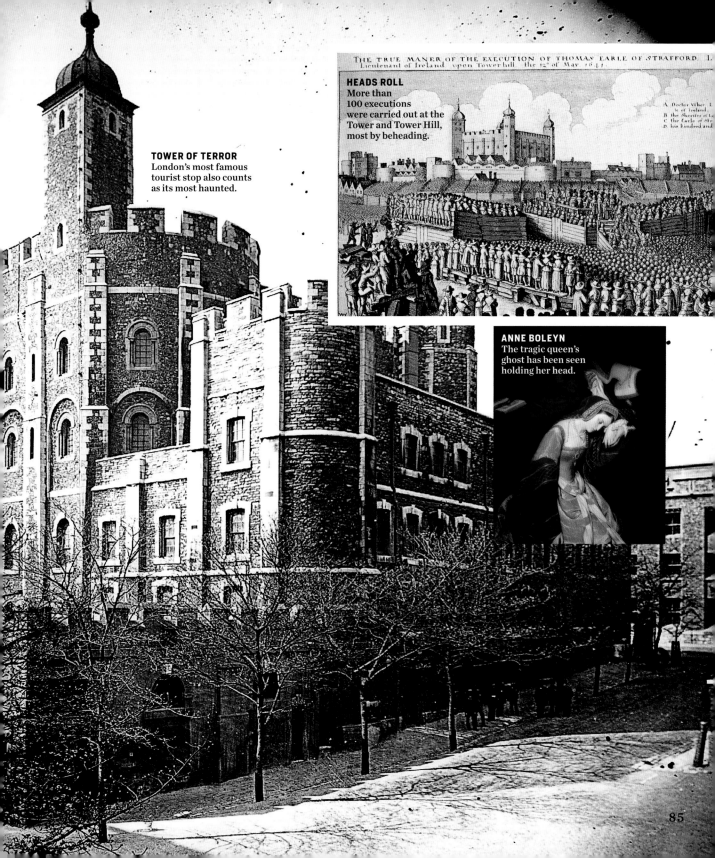

TOWER OF TERROR
London's most famous tourist stop also counts as its most haunted.

HEADS ROLL
More than 100 executions were carried out at the Tower and Tower Hill, most by beheading.

ANNE BOLEYN
The tragic queen's ghost has been seen holding her head.

PORCH VIOLENCE
A man shot outside
is said to haunt the
stairway where he died.

ST. FRANCISVILLE, LOUISIANA

MYRTLES PLANTATION

The spirits aren't camera-shy in this antebellum mansion of Southern splendor.

An innocuous-looking photograph at first glance, it was taken in 1992 for an insurance company to show the distance between two buildings for the purposes of writing up fire coverage.

But examine it more closely. There, in the breezeway between the General's Store and the Butler's Pantry, stands what looks like a woman in a dress with her head wrapped in a scarf or turban—yet no such woman works at the plantation now.

According to legend, a female in a turban *did* once live here—a slave named Chloe, who reportedly died amid scandal at the hand of fellow slaves. Did she return to the porch to pose for the camera?

A stately pre-Civil War mansion of ornamental ironwork, marble mantels and French gold-leaf furnishings, the Myrtles Plantation is said to be one of the most haunted places in the world, with reports of the nocturnal screams of children who aren't there, a piano that plays the same chord on its own, a Baccarat crystal chandelier that jangles in a room bereft of breeze, and beds that shake. A strange coolness wafts over the 17th step of the stairs, where a man shot outside on the veranda was said to have later collapsed and died.

The most famous ghost, though, is Chloe, who in life was said to be the governess for a judge's family, forced into having sex with him to keep her house job. When the judge tired of her, she feared she'd be sent to the fields, so she poisoned a birthday cake with oleander to get his children sick enough to require her care. But she misjudged the dose, and the mother and two daughters died. Concerned about guilt by association, other slaves lynched Chloe and tossed her body into the Mississippi River.

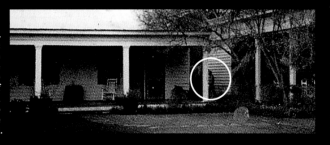

SPIRITUAL VISITOR The image in this photo has the same size and shape of a turbaned slave girl who may have been killed.

USS HORNET

Ghosts prowl the decks of a cavernous aircraft carrier that survived wars and storms.

After serving honorably for nearly three decades, surviving two wars and a typhoon, and recovering Apollo astronauts splashing down from moon missions, the *USS Hornet* aircraft carrier was decommissioned in 1970. The *Hornet* was declared a state and historic landmark and berthed in Oakland, where it opened for tours. But it seems some of its crew members are still reporting for duty. As many as 50 ghosts have been spotted wandering throughout this huge ship, haunting a vessel that saw more than its share of death during World War II and the Vietnam War.

Stories of unexplained phenomena and suddenly disappearing soldiers fill the *USS Hornet* Ghost Stories blog. "I heard a loud sound on the solid steel floor next to me, then the table thumped and moved slightly," writes one rattled

"I truly believe we saw a ghost."

Visitor whose camera was yanked away by an invisible force, in the Hornet's blog

man who brought a Scout troop to the ship for an overnighter. "I told no one, as to not frighten any boys."

Norene Balovich, the Bay Area–based host of the YouTube show *Paranormal Zone TV*, whose husband—a retired cop—works security on the *Hornet,* recalls how a specter appeared one night in her bedroom. "I couldn't see his face, but he had on that brown khaki uniform," says Balovich. "I just said, 'I'm so tired, please don't bother me, I want to go to sleep.' I've never seen him again." She thinks the ghost followed her husband home, though her doubting spouse didn't witness it.

STORM DAMAGE
A typhoon battered
the ship during WWII.

87

ENDLESS PASSAGES
The mansion has 160 rooms, 47 fireplaces, six kitchens and 40 stairways.

WINCHESTER HOUSE

A rich and depressed widow obsessively builds the world's strangest haunted mansion.

The death of gun magnate William Winchester in 1881 delivered a second blow to his wife, Sarah, who had never fully recovered from the loss of their infant daughter shortly after the child's birth 15 years earlier.

After inheriting $20.5 million and a half-stake in her husband's Winchester Repeating Arms Co., the devastated widow reportedly went to a medium for advice on how to use her riches to salvage her shattered life.

"You must start a new life and build a home for yourself and for the spirits who have fallen from this terrible weapon," the medium told her, according to legend. "You can never stop building the house. If you continue building, you will live. Stop, and you will die."

It was advice she was said to have followed to the point of obsession. Sarah moved from Connecticut to San Jose, California, where in about 1886 she started renovating a six-room house—and never stopped.

For nearly four decades, construction proceeded—at an often frantic pace, sometimes 24 hours a day—on what would become a world-famous architec-

Workers had no master plan and were guided by Sarah's ever-changing ideas. The Winchester House soon grew into a sprawling labyrinth of multiple styles. It has seven stories and more than 100 rooms, with new wings added against old windows, staircases rising to dead ends, and dozens of fireplaces, including one that didn't go all the way to the ceiling. Only Sarah Winchester's death in 1922 silenced the hammers.

Whether Sarah was truly driven by spirits or, as some historians argue, by a need to keep busy in the face of depression (or just to be left alone), the mansion has fascinated generations of visitors—it's open for tours—and inspired a 2018 movie, *Winchester*, starring Helen Mirren as Sarah Winchester.

Psychics report that Sarah's supposedly sad compulsions have triggered powerful paranormal vibes. Visitors claimed to hear voices and footsteps, banging doors and clattering windows.

Sarah herself has been said to make appearances now and then, perhaps irritated at the strangers in her home—or in search of the millions of dollars in gold that some say she hid

Mrs. Sarah Winchester - Only known portrait in existence. 1217

Sarah Winchester

Was she just misunderstood? Sarah Winchester may have been quirky, but many people believe she was completely sane. Historian Mary Jo Ignoffo suggests one reason for the constant construction was to discourage unwanted relatives from visiting.

CLEVELAND, OHIO

FRANKLIN CASTLE

A string of deaths is said to curse this ominous mansion with
a reputation for murder, spirits and a stash of hidden bones.

Even before old human bones were found in a closet there, Franklin Castle had a reputation for strange and frightening events.

Constructed in 1881 in what was one of Cleveland's most exclusive neighborhoods, this Queen Anne–style mansion adorned with gargoyles and turrets became home to the family of Hannes Tiedemann, a German immigrant who made a fortune in the barrel and banking businesses.

But Tiedmann's luck turned with the deaths of his 15-year-old daughter Emma and his elderly mother, which cast a pall over the magnificent Franklin Boulevard home. When his wife also died, people said the mansion was cursed—and that Tiedemann was a force of evil.

Tales were told of Tiedemann building secret tunnels and hidden rooms with sliding doors where he had sexual escapades, and even committed the murders of a mistress, a servant and an insane niece.

Though none of it was ever proved, the innuendo would forever follow Tiedemann and the mansion. As the house changed hands, there were whispers that it was used for bootlegging during Prohibition, as the headquarters for Nazi spies and that it was home to ghosts.

From visions of a woman in black to eerie noises, there have been reports of all sorts of paranormal activity, including organ music emanating from different rooms and human voices heard chattering in the old ballroom. A priest refused to perform an exorcism but confirmed an eerie presence. A Cleveland radio host claimed something yanked his recorder off his shoulder and tossed it down the stairs. One family believed their children were playing upstairs with the ghost of Emma Tiedemann.

In 1974, a new owner found a secret cabinet of old human bones. Authorities said these could have been medical specimens used by a doctor who once lived there. But others insisted these must have been the remains of Hannes Tiedemann's victims.

ALL IN THE FAMILY
Did a curse
fall upon the
Tiedemann clan?

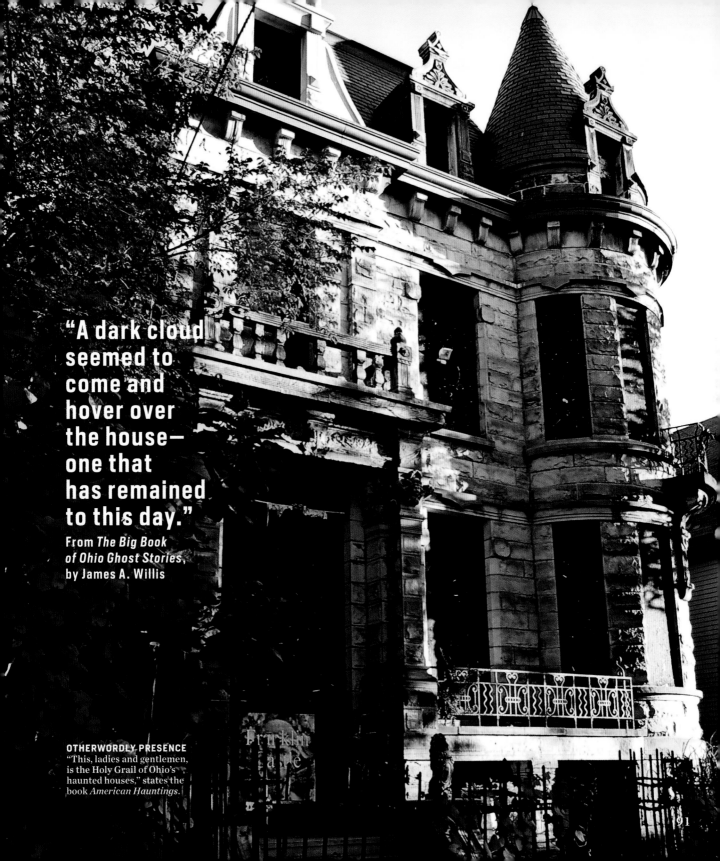

"A dark cloud seemed to come and hover over the house— one that has remained to this day."

From *The Big Book of Ohio Ghost Stories*, by James A. Willis

OTHERWORDLY PRESENCE
"This, ladies and gentlemen, is the Holy Grail of Ohio's haunted houses," states the book *American Hauntings*.

CLATSOP COUNTY, OREGON

TILLAMOOK ROCK LIGHTHOUSE

This beacon on a tiny rock off the coast of Oregon has been dark for 63 years.

A little more than a mile off the Oregon coast on an acre of basalt rock, Tillamook Rock Lighthouse stands amid the swirling Pacific waters, its light extinguished.

Described by its last keeper as "one of the most notorious and yet fascinating of the sea-swept sentinels in the world," the lighthouse was constructed over 575 difficult days, with at least one fatality linked to the project: Even before construction work began, a mason who was surveying the location was swept out to sea, his body never recovered.

The lighthouse began operation in 1881, guiding ships in the Columbia River around dangerous Tillamook Head—a run so harrowing, sailors nicknamed the lighthouse Terrible Tillie.

Four rotating keepers at a time were assigned to the remote location for three-month stints followed by two weeks off. That was later reduced to 42 days on and 21 days off, due to the harsh mental and physical conditions on the inhospitable rock.

It was decommissioned in 1957 and sold to private owners. Now empty, it is part of the Oregon Islands National Wildlife Refuge.

ROCKY LANDING
About a week before the lighthouse's completion, a ship crashed on its shore, killing all 16 crew members on board. Only the ship's dog survived.

The Smell of Fear

The churning waters could smash a boat to pieces, but it's no better if you make it ashore. "It's a popular rest place for birds. The guano there...the ammonia there would gag you," fisherman Scott Rekate told the *Daily Astorian*. "To start out to the top you'd have to take a deep breath and then run up the stairs."

HOLLYWOOD HORRORS

These spooky real-life locales offered filmmakers the chance to give audiences goosebumps, screams and shivers.

THE SHINING
STANLEY HOTEL

In the fall of 1974, writer Stephen King and his wife checked into this once-grand resort in Estes Park, Colorado, hoping a change of scenery would shake him out of a bad case of writer's block. With the hotel about to shut down for the winter, the Kings had the place almost to themselves. The creepy solitude of the old, empty edifice—and unexplained sounds—inspired him to write *The Shining*, the best-selling novel later adapted to the blockbuster film.

The hotel reportedly received visitors from the beyond almost from the moment it opened. In 1911, a maid carried a candle into a room where gas was leaking. The subsequent explosion injured but didn't kill her, yet for decades Room 217 has been said to be haunted by a spirit who pesters guests. It also happens to be the same room where King spent the night.

CHECKING IN
The Torrance family in *The Shining* head out for a haunting time.

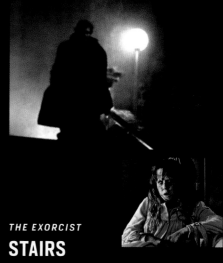

THE TEXAS CHAIN SAW MASSACRE
THE GAS STATION

The sign outside the store reads "We slaughter barbecue"—which must come as a welcome relief, considering what was killed here in *The Texas Chain Saw Massacre*. The backwoods service station where power tool–wielding cannibals served chili made from humans had hit hard times after the 1974 cult classic was released, opening and closing under different names. Now restored, the newly named The Gas Station in Bastrop, Texas, 40 miles southeast of Austin, embraces its horror film past, selling memorabilia and autographed photos of the film's star Caroline Williams.

THE EXORCIST
STAIRS

At the climax of *The Exorcist*, Father Damien Karras crashes out of a window and tumbles down a steep flight of outdoor stairs to his death. To get the scene right, a stuntman had to fall down the stairs twice, his body protected by half-inch rubber on the steps. These stairs in the Georgetown section of Washington, D.C., are more likely to attract joggers than demon-possessed priests. But the location's significance isn't lost on the locals: The "*Exorcist* stairs" are recognized as an official D.C. landmark.

FRIDAY THE 13TH
CAMP CRYSTAL LAKE

The watchtower is still there. So are the archery range, pond and counselor cabin. But the only Jasons running around are young guys working on their merit badges. Camp Crystal Lake from *Friday the 13th* is in fact a real-life camp. Run by the Boy Scouts of America as Camp No-Be-Bo-Sco, the 300-acre camp in northwestern New Jersey has been welcoming Scouts since 1927. Although the movie's characters came to dreadful ends, the scariest thing about the real camp is the warning on the website: "Please note that the camp is private property and is NOT open to the public for visiting or tours." This policy does occasionally relax, with the establishment offering a public tour scheduled, naturally, on Friday the 13th.

GHOST TOWNS

SPIRITS TAKE UP
RESIDENCE IN THESE
DESERTED TOWNS
EMPTIED BY WAR,
DISASTER AND DESPAIR.

UKRAINE

PRIPYAT

The Chernobyl disaster turned the bustling city into a postapocalyptic time capsule.

Once Pripyat pulsed with life, theaters, stores, factories, a hospital, even an amusement park. Then on April 26, 1986, during a routine test, reactor 4 at the Chernobyl nuclear station, 2 miles away, exploded and caught fire. Two workers were killed in the blast and 28 firemen and emergency workers died in the next three months after being exposed to the radioactive material.

Evacuations were ordered for the entire town of Pripyat, population 49,360. People scooped up whatever they could carry and fled, leaving behind a haunting time capsule.

Soviet propaganda posters hang from peeling walls. Children's schoolbooks remain cracked open on dusty desks. Yellow gondolas dangle empty on a Ferris wheel, and the bumper cars sit forever idle. Old gas masks lie in piles next to yel-

lowing instruction manuals. The concrete apartment buildings stand eerily silent, the windows broken, the plazas deserted and overgrown with weeds and trees. The clocks are all stopped at 11:55 a.m., when electricity was cut off.

For decades, Pripyat served as a terrible symbol of the horrors the Chernobyl disaster wrought, with thousands of deaths from radiation-related cancers. The city now is a symbol of a differ-

Scary Creatures

While they aren't glowing in the dark, Pripyat's animals were genetically altered by the fallout. Birds have been found with smaller brains, some barn swallows developed albinism, giant wild boars have been spotted and there are reports of unusually aggressive wolves prowling nearby villages.

LEFT TO ROT
To avoid radioactive contamination, visitors to Pripyat are warned not to take anything from the city, or to sit down or touch anything.

ent sort, showing what the world may look like after humans are gone.

Pripyat and its environs have in some ways yielded back to nature. While the ecosystem still shows scars of radiation, foxes, wolves, raccoons and dogs scamper about and bison and brown bears are present. This phenomenon, plus the macabre spectacle of the abandoned city, has turned Pripyat into a tourist draw, as radiation reaches safer levels.

ABANDONED
Fear of bubonic plague condemned the Underground in 1907.

Out for Justice

Edward isn't Pioneer Square's only ghost. In 1882, a mob lynched two men who had been accused of murdering businessman George Reynolds. The bloodthirsty crowd then stormed the local jail and dragged another prisoner, Benjamin Payne, to the gallows. Just before dying, Payne told them, "You hang me, and you will hang an innocent man." Ever since, there have been sightings of a ghost with a broken neck.

SEATTLE UNDERGROUND

An eerie subterranean city takes visitors deep into the land's past.

Beneath the sidewalks of Seattle lurks a secret second city of dark corridors and abandoned 1800s storefronts for a butcher shop, bank, bars and merchants, frozen in time like Pompeii.

The Seattle Underground came about because of the Great Seattle Fire of 1889, which wiped out 25 blocks of mostly wood buildings and spurred city officials to solve two nagging problems. They ordered new structures to be built out of brick and masonry. And they raised the city—literally.

Along with the constant fire danger, Seattle's Pioneer Square, originally built on low tideland fill, would flood and turn the streets into a sea of sticky mud.

There are tales of dogs and small children being sucked into the muck.

After the fire, retaining walls went up and the streets were raised. This left deep walkways between the walls and buildings, many of which were rebuilt in haste to ride the late-1880s financial boom. The walkways were no longer used, and the lower floors of the buildings now lay underground, creating a dark and parallel city of flophouses, opium dens and speakeasies.

As the above-ground area deteriorated over the years, losing residents and business to uptown, the eerie subterranean treasures remained unseen and unknown to most. Then in the 1960s, an irreverent local writer named Bill Speidel, who long advocated preserving the historic birthplace of the city, started giving underground tours.

The neighborhood is now the trendy old town district, and the Underground is a popular tourist destination, with multiple groups offering guided tours.

Along the way, visitors may meet the Underground's ghostly greeter, Edward, a teller in an abandoned bank that has long loomed in darkness. Edward would store miners' gold in the vault, until he was shot and killed during a robbery. Still sporting a top hat, handlebar mustache and suspenders, Edward has been known to chat with visitors from the land of the living before promptly disappearing without so much as a goodbye.

ON LOCATION *The Night Strangler* with Darren McGavin is a movie about the Underground.

HIGH AND DRY Buildings went up and so did the streets after the Great Fire.

PENNSYLVANIA

CENTRALIA

An underground fire that has burned for decades dooms a small town.

It was a decision that would sound the death knell for an entire town. In 1962, an intentionally set fire in a landfill that used to be a strip-mining pit spread to coal-filled mining tunnels deep below the ground—and kept on burning. Toxic fumes shot out of hundreds of holes opened in the griddle-hot surface, choking many of the 1,000 residents of Centralia, Pennsylvania, out of their homes. Huge swaths of land lost vegetation, and trees died off, leaving white-bleached ghost stumps. The ground got so hot that plastic bottles melted and cracks opened up straight down Highway 61. A 12-year-old boy fell into a steaming hole.

But fighting a fire 300 feet underground proved technically and economically impossible, and so it continued to smolder for decades. By the early 1980s, officials gave up. "Pennsylvania didn't have enough money in the bank to do the job," Steve Jones, a geologist with the state's Office of Surface Mining, told *Smithsonian Magazine*. "If you aren't going to put it out, what can you do? Move the people."

And with millions of dollars in relocation funds, most of the residents of this once proud and thriving community did just that: They went elsewhere, leaving behind a hellscape of noxious odors and razed houses. A dozen or so stubborn souls refused to go; the rest aren't coming back. Officials say there's enough underground coal left to keep the fire burning for another 200 years.

WHERE THERE'S SMOKE
Fire raged underground for decades.

FAULT LINES
As the blame
game raged,
so did the fire.

"[Temperatures] reached over 900 degrees F in some locations."

History.com

FAMAGUSTA, CYPRUS

VAROSHA & NICOSIA

Celebrities once played at these now bombed-
out sites on this Mediterranean island.

When the Turkish army invaded the island of Cyprus in 1974, tens of thousands of residents fled Varosha, the popular resort spot in the city of Famagusta, with little more than the clothes on their backs. Overnight, the tourist destination—where Elizabeth Taylor vacationed and Brigitte Bardot and Raquel Welch shopped fashionable boutiques—was a ghost town.

Today, the area is a grim symbol of divided rule. The resort suffered major bombing damage before it was surrounded by a barbed-wire fence and barred entry to everyone except Turkish soldiers and United Nations personnel for more than four decades. The area has remained almost exactly as it was, down to the cars in dealer showrooms.

The same fate awaited the Nicosia International Airport west of the Cypriot capital, Nicosia. Used as a military airfield since the 1930s, the airport expanded to include a modern terminal for commercial flights capable of handling 800 passengers a day. Then Turkish forces bombed the airport and its hangars and waiting rooms. A lone Cyprus Airways Trident Sun Jet passenger plane sits sadly on the tarmac, awaiting takeoff clearance that will never come. The airport now serves as the headquarters of

A Return to Glory?

As recently as 2019, the Turkish foreign minister announced that "preparations are being made" to reopen the fenced-off resort, and the Turkish–Cypriot prime minister declared Varosha "will become Las Vegas again." Cyprus immediately denounced the plans as a violation of the UN resolutions, with the president of the Republic of Cyprus calling it "completely unacceptable."

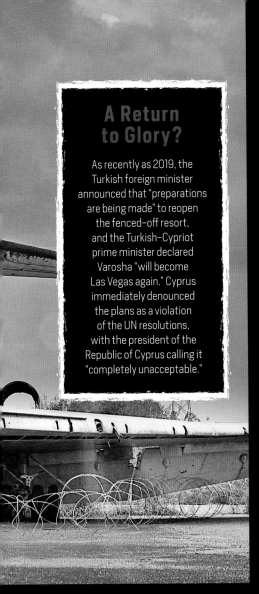

BEFORE
The rich and famous enjoyed the beaches and shops.

"The picture that I had in my mind was a kind of paradise. But it felt like some sort of postapocalyptic nightmare."

Former Varosha resident Vasia Markides, telling the BBC about seeing her home for the first time in decades

YASAK BÖLGE GİRİLMEZ

FORBIDDEN ZONE

ZONE INTERDITE

VERBOTENE ZONE

ΑΠΑΓΩΡΕΥΜΕΝΗ ΖΩΝΗ
ΑΠΑΓΩΡΕΥΕΤΑΙ Η ΕΙΣΟΔΟΣ

the UN Peacekeeping Force, and a place for intermittent talks to find a solution to the political impasse.

As Turkish and Greek Cypriot officials bicker over the fate of the Forbidden Zone, its buildings continue to crumble. A 1984 UN resolution states the city can only be resettled by its original residents, and activists hope to restore Varosha to its former glory even after suffering decades of decay.

AFTER
Buildings stand gutted and abandoned.

JAPAN

HASHIMA ISLAND

Once one of the most densely populated areas in the world, this Japanese location is now abandoned.

A tiny island of deserted buildings in the middle of the ocean, this grim location looks like the kind of place where a James Bond villain would hole up while plotting world domination. Indeed, the producers of 2012's *Skyfall* saw the potential in Japan's Hashima Island, and used it as a location for the film.

Japan owes much of its industrial growth to this 16-acre island located 9 miles off its southwestern coast. For nearly 100 years, coal was mined in underwater tunnels by forced labor, and at its peak in 1959 more than 5,200 people were crammed into 10-story apartments in a city protected by a sea wall.

As the coal ran out in the 1970s, the mines were shut down and the island was deserted, leaving behind the complex of housing, schools, shops, restaurants and gambling houses blanketing every inch of what locals called Midori nashi Shima—the island without green. The island has since become a popular tourist attraction for its well-preserved ghost city.

NOT FORGOTTEN
The island
was deemed a
UNESCO World
Heritage Site
in 2015.

"Stepping off the boat is
like entering a dystopian world
of sci-fi or video games."
Lonely Planet

ITALY

VILLAGE OF CRACO

A hillside town in Italy survived a plague—only to fall victim to landslides and an earthquake.

Perched on a cliff 1,300 feet over Italy's Cavone River valley, near the instep of the "boot" of Italy, this ancient settlement was perfectly positioned to defend itself against invaders since its founding by Greeks in the eighth century B.C. Growing into a military center and picturesque village dominated by a castle built in 1300, Craco endured centuries of change, as well as a plague in 1656 that killed hundreds and reduced the population significantly. But it couldn't withstand the forces of nature and the soft ground on which it sits.

A series of landslides in the early 1960s forced many residents from their homes. Periodic earthquakes only added to the danger. After a flood in 1972 and an earthquake in 1980, the medieval village was deserted, with the residents forced to live in tent cities as they searched for housing options.

Today, Craco has enjoyed new life hosting religious and music festivals. It's also served as a movie location for films, including *The Passion of the Christ* and *Quantum of Solace*, and is the focus of conservation efforts to maintain the site and its history.

DRAWING CROWDS
People flock to Craco for festivals paying homage to the Virgin Mary.

"Dark windows
look out…
like empty eye
sockets."
Ancient-Origins.net

TOWERING VIEW
The village's
oldest building,
the Norman
Tower, was
built in 1040.

BARREN
SURROUNDINGS
A town built
with sweat
and blood now
crumbles.

ALASKA
KENNECOTT

A copper-mining town born in short order
in the Alaskan wilds dies just as quickly.

In 1900, two prospectors exploring a glacier in eastern Alaska hit upon the richest copper deposit ever found: Mountain cliffs had turned green from the exposed, oxidized mineral. Copper was valued at the time for its use in the new technologies of electricity and telephones, so the find was as good as gold. It brought with it, however, good times that inevitably couldn't last and tragedy that would be felt forever.

Within seven years, the mining town of Kennecott had sprung up in the Alaskan wilds, connected to a 200-mile railroad that brought copper ore south to Prince William Sound, where it was shipped to smelters in Tacoma, Washington. Financed by J.P. Morgan, the railroad was an engineering marvel, the tracks having to be constantly adjusted because they spanned shifting glaciers.

Nobody knows for certain how many of the thousands of workers died from explosions, avalanches and exposure while creating the railroad. By the 1930s, the copper had eventually given out, and Kennecott was abandoned.

Visitors who slog 300 miles east of Anchorage to the old mines and town claim to have heard the cries of those lost laborers.

It's so spooky that in the late 1990s, the state of Alaska struggled to develop government housing along the old railroad grade. Construction workers were so rattled by visions of phantoms and disembodied voices, according to the *Anchorage Daily News*, that "keeping work up became impossible."

DOWNWARD SPIRAL As copper prices collapsed, so did the town.

Workers then started mysteriously losing their tools, even those in their belts. "It was enough to frighten off even the boldest and bravest public servant," the *Anchorage Daily News* reported, "and the whole project is said to have been canceled."

Today, the former railroad grade is a hiking trail to the old town of Kennecott, an attraction operated by the National Park Service, which is renovating some of the buildings.

ALABAMA

CAHAWBA

A ghost tried to warn this once-thriving Southern town that its days were numbered.

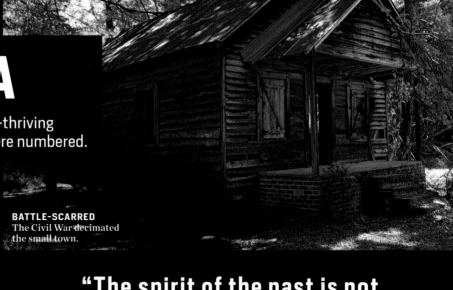

BATTLE-SCARRED
The Civil War decimated the small town.

The famous flying ghost first floated into view during the Civil War. A Confederate soldier headed for duty spent one last evening with his sweetheart strolling under the moonlight through the most romantic spot in town, a garden maze of cedars at the home of one Colonel C. C. Pegues.

"A large, white glowing ball darted toward them," according to the book *Thirteen Alabama Ghosts and Jeffrey.* "It appeared to be floating in the air a few feet above the ground as though controlled by a powerful but invisible force."

Once the bustling capital of Alabama, the low-lying town kept flooding, and the statehouse was moved to Tuscaloosa. The Civil War finished it off. Ruins and spirits are all that's left.

Although Pegues' home was demolished, "Pegues' Ghost" is said to still make regular appearances in the cedars near where the house stood. Some insist the ghost is a message sent by Pegues himself—who died fighting the Battle of Gaines' Mill in Virginia—warning of the dangers of war or signaling that the entire town would one day die. "Cahawba, like the Pegues' Ghost, was soon to become immaterial, a place owing more to the past than the future, a place inhabited primarily by the events of its former glory days," says the town's website.

> ## "The spirit of the past is not going to hold still."
> Site manager Linda Derry, in *The New York Times*

RESTING PLACES
Slaves and white people are buried in separate cemeteries.

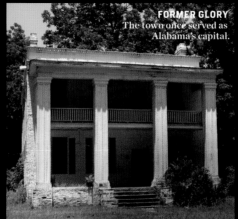

FORMER GLORY
The town once served as Alabama's capital.

GHOST STORIES
Tales of spirits date to the 1800s.

DARK HISTORY
Did evil forces drive residents to insanity and suicide?

Deadly curse turned New England village into a ghost town!

An incredibly deadly, centuries-old curse wiped out the once-thriving New England village of Dudleytown, Conn., driving residents to suicide and madness and causing others to die mysteriously, say researchers.

Madness, death & accidents wiped out the residents

Today the site of Dudleytown is an uninhabited ghost town, with only crumbling stone foundations of buildings still remaining as a reminder of the village's tragic history.

There is absolutely no question that Dudleytown was destroyed by the Dudley Curse," said world-famed psychic researcher Ed Warren.

Warren said that according to local legends, events celebrated in 1510 when an Englishman named Edmund Dudley was beheaded for plotting to overthrow the king of England. Satanists in the royal court placed the curse on the Dudley family.

A great-grandson, William Dudley, came to America in 1630. Approximately 100 years later four of his descendant founded Dudleytown.

By the early 1800s Dudleytown was a bustling community of several hundred people, boasting two schools, a church, a general store and a blacksmith shop.

But even as the village grew, the Dudley Curse was already taking its deadly toll. In 1774, six members of the Carter family, who had settled in Dudleytown, died from cholera.

"About the same time, Abviel Dudley, oldest of the four founding brothers, went mad, raving that he saw weird animals and terrifying green creatures," Warren said.

"He remained insane until his death."

In 1792, a Dudleytown resident, Gershon Hollister, was found brutally murdered at the home of William Tanner—who was also babbling insanely about demonic creatures. He remained insane until he died.

In 1804, lightning killed Sarah Gaye Swift, wife of one of Dudleytown's most prominent citizens, General Herman Swift.

"When Gen. Swift learned his wife's death, he went

MRS. DAVID
Psychic Astrologer
Foresees future events through birthdate. High powered psychic, she has the ability to help and solve all problems. Career changes, relationships, business, family, love, health based on birthdate information. See into your future. Send $5.00 and self addressed envelope. Name, date of birth. Free energy crystal with each reading.
182 Elkton Rd.
Newark, Del. 19711
(302) 456-5793
Money back guarantee.

DESERTED Dudleytown is located in Connecticut.

CONNECTICUT

DUDLEYTOWN

A nobleman loses his head and gains a curse that is said to follow his family to America.

According to legend, Dudleytown's troubles date to 1510, when a British nobleman named Edmund Dudley plotted to overthrow King Henry VIII. His Royal Highness, not known to be forgiving in such situations, separated Dudley from his head, and as an added punishment he had a powerful curse placed upon his family. This curse, it has been said, followed Dudley's descendants to the New World in the 1700s, all the way to the forest where they settled, in what is now northwestern Connecticut.

Dudleytown's population was only a few dozen people, and the enclave comprised small houses of farmers struggling to grow crops in the rocky soil in a deep valley called Dark Entry Forest. (The ominous name comes from the long shadows cast by the surrounding mountains.) The discovery of iron ore kept the town going, and New Yorkers would trickle in for the country life.

But by the 1940s, much of the town had been abandoned, the people driven out by strange and awful forces. Vicious creatures were said to emerge from the trees and make people insane. Illness and suicide seemed to afflict nearly everybody who lived in or near Dudleytown. Screams came from the woods; orbs darted among the branches; crops wouldn't grow; birds wouldn't sing.

Curiosity-seekers flocked to the townsite, hoping to feel the vortex of evil. Nearly every story has been debunked (there's no evidence the British Dudleys are even related to the town settlers), and this private property is marked with "no trespassing" signs—but still, they visit. Ruins have been vandalized and beer cans tossed around, and the police are constantly called to shoo people away. It appears Dudleytown has been hit by something even more powerful than a kingly curse: the sting of notoriety.

DERINKUYU UNDERGROUND CITY

An ancient haven beneath the surface protected residents from marauding armies.

During the 1963 renovation of a home in the Anatolia region of Turkey, a wall caved in, exposing what at first looked like a basement but instead turned out to be a portal to an incredible ancient underground city. Carved out of soft volcanic rock about 250 feet down sometime before 1200 B.C., this 18-story subterranean metropolis consisted of homes, schools, stables, armories, wells and tombs that sheltered up to 20,000 people and their livestock, including goats and sheep.

Used over the centuries by people hiding from invasions and war—and also likely seeking refuge from the blistering summer heat—the multilevel underground city was accessed by secret tunnels with ladders, the rooms connected by a maze of passageways and ventilated by dozens of air shafts. It may even be connected to another underground city located five miles away. In 1969, after an extensive excavation, about half of the city was opened to visitors.

GIVE ME SHELTER
Derinkuyu was used as a hideout by residents of a local town during the Armenian massacre in 1909.

"The landscape looks like something out of *Mad Max*."
LA Weekly

CALIFORNIA

SALTON RIVIERA

A popular Golden State lakeside resort dies a long, stinky death as Salton Sea water levels sink.

In the 1950s and 1960s, the sunny shores of California's largest lake sparkled as a glamorous playground where Frank Sinatra, Jerry Lewis and members of The Beach Boys stayed in fancy hotels and launched their yachts from the marina at Bombay Beach.

The Salton Riviera, as it was known, was born by accident. In 1905, heavy spring water flow from the Colorado River overwhelmed agricultural irrigation canals and poured into an ancient dry lake bed, creating the Salton Sea. Located just an hour from Palm Springs, the lake became a popular getaway. But over the years, Salton Sea—with no natural outflow—became too salty and polluted with fertilizer runoff from the surrounding farmlands. Algae blooms exploded, and dead fish began to wash ashore in vast, rotting piles. The dead algae sinking to the bottom feeds a bacteria that produced hydrogen sulfide gas, which can be as deadly as cyanide.

By the 1970s, the nasty water and stench scared away the tourists, and the resort area became a dusty shell of itself, with only a handful of businesses surviving. The smell today is so bad that odor advisories are issued for the entire Coachella Valley downwind. The Salton Sea Authority passed a resolution in 2019 declaring a state of emergency, in the hopes of getting funding to replenish the water from the Sea of Cortez in Mexico. Until then, this onetime desert gem is deteriorating into what Bombay Beach bartender Steven Johnson described, in an NPR interview, as a "slow-motion apocalypse."

SLOW DECLINE
(From top) Residents fled the stench and pollution; fish suffocated in the oxygen-starved lake; the tanking economy emptied neighborhoods.

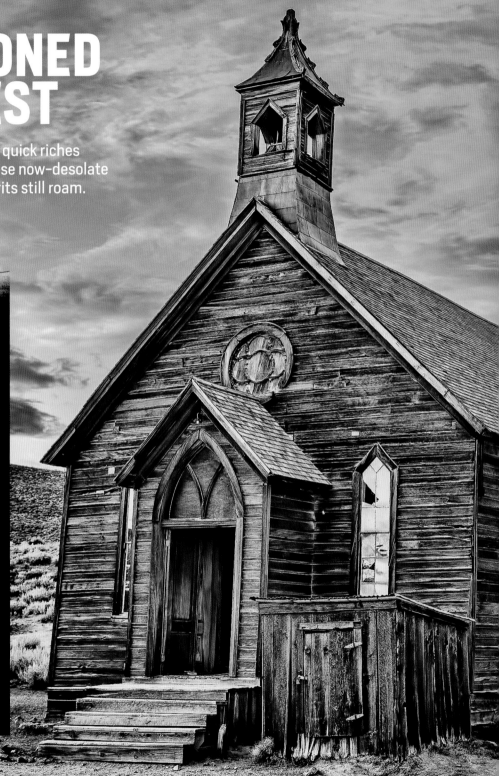

ABANDONED OUT WEST

The lure of gold and other quick riches brought thousands to these now-desolate towns where only the spirits still roam.

CALIFORNIA

BODIE

Once a dusty, remote mining camp, Bodie blossomed into a California boomtown with the discovery of rich gold-bearing ore in 1876. As the population exploded from a handful of prospectors to 7,000 miners, merchants, railroad workers, drifters, gamblers, robbers and gunslingers, as many as 65 saloons lined Main Street. Opium dens soon popped up and prostitutes plied their trade in the red-light district.

The many barroom fights and shoot-outs brought steady business to the mortuary, the town's only brick building—the other 2,000 structures were made of wood—and supplied enough corpses for two cemeteries: an official city cemetery and another for less-desirables.

After millions of dollars were extracted from the ground, the gold began to run out and miners fled for more promising stakes. By 1910, Bodie was nearly deserted, and it remained that way until it became a National Historic Landmark District in 1961.

CALIFORNIA
CERRO GORDO

The lead and silver extracted in the 19th century from Cerro Gordo ("fat hill" in Spanish), 9,000 feet above the Owens Valley in eastern California, was sent by mule train to the port of Los Angeles in an economic boost for the little pueblo. After mining fizzled out in the early 1900s, Cerro Gordo was abandoned to the elements and, some say, the ghosts—including the specter of a square-jawed man with deep-set eyes known to peer through the window of the restored American Hotel.

ARIZONA
VULTURE CITY

The most productive mine in Arizona history—it pumped out silver and gold worth $200 million from 1863 to 1942—spawned a town of 5,000 with saloons, brothels, general stores, a school, blacksmith and a notorious ironwood tree from which 18 men were hanged for their transgressions. The mine's closure in World War II doomed the town, and now the rickety buildings, never constructed to last, welcome visitors for a fee.

TEXAS
GLENRIO

Straddling the Texas/New Mexico border, Glenrio had a hardware store, cafés, a hotel and a quirky bifurcated existence: The bars were on the New Mexico side, because the Texas side was dry, and the service stations were also on the New Mexico side, since its gasoline taxes were lower than Texas'.

Established in 1903, Glenrio had few permanent residents but a healthy economy, thanks to Route 66. Midway between Chicago and Los Angeles, this humble hamlet became a convenient stop for cross-country travelers looking for a fill-up, a cold Coke or an overnight stay. But the 1950s closure of the railroad depot hobbled Glenrio, and the subsequent building of Interstate 40, which bypassed the town, was the final death blow.

THE MYSTERIOUS OUTDOORS

VENTURE—IF YOU DARE—INTO THESE FORESTS, ISLANDS AND RIVERS WHERE MOTHER NATURE PROVIDES NO PROTECTION.

XOCHIMILCO CANALS, MEXICO

ISLAND OF THE DOLLS

Thousands of dolls hung by an obsessed man terrify visitors.

A two-hour boat ride south of Mexico City, through the lily pad–covered canals, takes visitors to a place where the dolls are so scary Chucky would run screaming. Everywhere, there are dolls by the thousands, hanging by wires from trees, impaled on branches, dismembered and decapitated, crawling with ants, covered in spiderwebs, and splashed with mud and blood-red paint. The macabre spectacle is the fruit of the obsessions of the island's former caretaker, Don Julian Santa Barrera.

According to the local legend, he discovered a little drowned girl in the canal in 1951, followed shortly by a doll floating nearby. As a tribute to the child's spirit, or out of guilt for failing to save her life, he began hanging dolls from the trees, and never stopped for the next half-century. With no hard evidence corroborating the story of the child's death, some say that Barrera, driven mad by loneliness or the loss of a girlfriend to another man—or both—invented the story to explain his bizarre hobby. For whatever reason, year after year, dolls of all shapes and sizes and designs, their eyes sometimes gouged out, were strung around the island, until Barrera died in 2001, reportedly drowning in the same spot where he'd found the girl.

The Island of the Dolls brings chills to visitors, many of whom insist the dolls have taken on lives of their own, especially at night, when the dolls are said to whisper, blink, and wiggle their arms and legs. It's so scary that when visitors get home they'll never look at Barbie the same way again. Locals aren't so frightened. In fact, many consider the island charmed, not haunted. Maybe that's because the Island of Dolls has become a major money-earning tourist destination.

GRIEVING
Did a child's death drive a man to hang dolls for 50 years?

PINE BARRENS

A monster of myth terrorizes a dense forest and gives a pro hockey team its mascot.

Normally, tracks in the snow don't make headlines. But in January 1909, the *Asbury Park Press* in New Jersey reported: "Jersey Fields and Yards, Covered by Imprints of a Two-Legged Something." Suffice it to say, nobody thought a human left those tracks—or any sort of normal animal.

Many feared that this was the work of the monstrous red-eyed, horned, flying, feathered beast with bat wings, hooves and claws known as the Jersey Devil, which usually makes its home in the dark woods of the Pine Barrens, 1.1 million acres over seven counties. It's a legend that survives to this day.

Posses were formed to find and kill the beast, but their bloodhounds refused to follow the tracks. Schools and mills shut their doors, residents cowered in their homes and a $250,000 bounty was put on the Devil's head.

Each report was more frantic. Police fired guns at the Devil in Camden and Bristol. A trolley was attacked. Chickens and dogs were eaten. One fisherman claimed to have fought the Devil in a "fierce battle" off the Jersey Shore, showing bruised arms and a shredded coat as proof.

According to local legend, a Pine Barrens woman known as Mother Leeds was so exasperated at getting pregnant for the 13th time that she told her drunken husband, "Let this one be a devil!"

Sure enough, the midwife helped deliver a monster born with hair and feathers and horns that killed Mother Leeds, the midwife, the father and their other children before flying up the chimney and inflicting 300 more years of mayhem.

The Jersey Devil, also known as the Leeds Devil, has become more than just a figure of local myth. It also inspired the state's professional hockey team, the Devils.

DEVIL'S REVENGE
The old mines and mills are also said to be haunted.

"You could
hear it coming
down the roof,
making these
click-clack,
weird metallic,
booming noises."
Witness Laurie Winkelmann,
History Channel

FURIOUS FLIGHT
The Leeds Devil is said to
swoop down from trees.

CURSED PLOT
Disaster struck in 1915 just
after a voodoo priestess died.

MANCHAC SWAMP

Ghostly legends are as thick as mosquitoes in the home of a voodoo princess.

Alligators peer out from the green ooze, and the moss hangs from the ancient cypress trees like a widow's veil. On the banks of the Manchac Swamp, northwest of New Orleans, the old shacks stand listlessly, long abandoned.

Or are they? Listen carefully and you might still hear her, the scary old lady strumming her guitar on a porch, singing a haunting prophesy of doom.

She once was a real person who called this primordial world home in the late 19th century. She's identified variously as Julie White and Julie Black. Research by *Mental Floss* found records showing she may have been Julia Brown, once married to a laborer. She spent her remaining days in their 40-acre homestead after he died.

Local legend gives her another name: The Big Bad. She's described as one of many voodoo priestesses lurking in Louisiana in the late 1800s, and she likely worked as a midwife and folk healer, as there were no doctors.

By 1915, she was as mean as the snakes slithering through the muck, singing her promises that she would soon die and take the town with her. Sure enough, Brown would pass away,

and on the day of her funeral, "many pranks were played by wind and tide," the *New Orleans Times-Picayune* reported at the time.

A powerful hurricane packing 125 mph winds soon blasted through the region, bringing a storm surge that wiped out the swamp towns and killed a large number of people. Had Brown made good on her curse? Or was she simply issuing a warning?

Her legend is one of many stories of the supernatural that drift through the swamp like fog. This land is also said to be the hunting grounds of Rougarou, the Cajun werewolf, a hairy 10-foot-tall monster with glowing red eyes and fangs. Sometimes it looks like a pig, sometimes like a bull, chasing away strangers and looking for blood.

OMINOUS NOTES
The warnings were sung from a shack's porch.

"One day I'm going to die and take the whole town with me."

Song of voodoo priestess Julia Brown

NAMIBIA

KOLMANSKOP MINING TOWN

Sandstorms have consumed the former diamond-mining area in the Namib Desert.

I n 1908, a Namibian railroad worker clearing sand off the rails spotted strange shimmering stones. He showed them to his supervisor, who had them inspected.

The stones were diamonds. The discovery transformed these sand dunes in West Africa's Namib Desert into the world's richest diamond mines, producing up to 1 million carats a year by 1912.

The little German colony town of Kolmanskop in southern Namibia blossomed into a diamond of its own, a surreal speck of luxury in the desert, nourished by fresh water brought by rail and entertained by visiting European opera troupes. German authorities sealed off the area into a Sperrgebiet, or restricted zone, and local tribespeople were displaced from their own land or left no choice but to work there as laborers.

When the diamonds ran out in the 1930s, miners moved on to more promising deposits, and by 1956 Kolmanskop was abandoned. As the desert reclaimed the land, mountains of sand invaded emptied buildings.

BLOWN AWAY
About 35,000 tourists visit Kolmanskop each year to explore the town, which in its heyday was home to about 1,000 people—including a family that kept a pet ostrich.

HOME BASE
The African town was built in
the architectural style
of a German village.

"The temple is the heart and soul of Cambodia."
The Lonely Planet

Picture Perfect

The most famous film shot at Angkor Wat is 2001's *Lara Croft: Tomb Raider*, starring Angelina Jolie. The temple's conservation authority charged Paramount Pictures $10,000 a day to shoot at the fragile site—a fortune in Cambodia. The success of the movie brought Angkor Wat new fame, which led to a rise in tourism.

ANGKOR WAT

A Cambodian complex that brought Hindu myths to life rose, then fell, before rediscovery.

Built in the early 12th century by a Khmer king, who, legend has it, murdered his great-uncle to rise to power, the Angkor Wat complex in Cambodia replicates the cosmos in stone: Its five towers represent Hindu mythology's Mount Meru and its peaks.

One of the world's largest and most elaborate religious monuments, Angkor Wat—which translates as "temple city"—stretches over 500 acres dominated by its 213-foot central tower and surrounded by a 13-foot-deep moat. Virtually every surface inside the temple is adorned with ornate carved images of gods, mythological scenes and dancers.

Dedicated to the deity Vishnu, often described as the "preserver" and "protector," Angkor Wat was later transformed into a Buddhist temple and teh region loomed as the largest city in the world at the time—with as many as 1 million people in the power center of the mighty Khmer Empire, which ruled much of Southeast Asia.

But by the early 15th century, Angkor Wat was abandoned and swallowed by the jungle; the cause is still debated, though it likely suffered a slow decline over a century, possibly as climate change disrupted rainfall and upended the water system. It would take the name "lost city" from Westerners, though locals always knew it was there.

Named a UNESCO World Heritage Site in 1992, it stands as Cambodia's most popular tourist attraction, an edifice as mighty as it is fragile.

If a stubborn drought in Cambodia lowers the waterline of the famed moat, the temple's sandstone foundations could suffer from exposure and compromise the integrity of the structures. Officials say evaporation is high, but the water supply is being regulated to protect the temple. "We have not ignored the issue," one official says.

Another concern is the aptly named strangler fig trees that took root in the loosened stones of the complex's temples, which were built without mortar.

Some of the trees at Angkor's smaller Ta Prohm temple had to be removed in order to stabilize the building and prevent the roots from further crushing the structure.

GROWING TROUBLE
The tree roots extract moisture from the sandstone, making it more prone to crumbling.

WHAT'S THAT SOUND?
Hikers hear a disembodied voice pleading, "Help me!"

CLAREMONT, CALIFORNIA

THOMPSON CREEK TRAIL

Leave suburbia behind for a chilling nighttime stroll.

A 5-mile loop on a paved path, Thompson Creek Trail takes hikers through a pleasant section of Southern California where the suburbs meet nature.

Popular with joggers, dog walkers and parents with kids in strollers, the trail runs behind the backyards of homes with horses and sheep. Deer forage in the brush. Lizards skitter across the path. The view of the San Gabriel Mountains is spectacular.

Hikers are warned to be on the lookout for mountain lions and rattlesnakes, and in the summer the heat can be intense. But otherwise the trail is considered a great place to spend a quiet Saturday, or to unwind after work.

But when the sun goes down, Thompson Creek Trail is said to become a much scarier place. "Visitors say they have seen shadowy figures following them and heard the crackling of branches, footsteps and scratching noises," according to the website Haunted Places.

The trail begins off the road to Mount Baldy on the fringes of the community of Claremont, east of Los Angeles. The power lines were "buzzing like crazy," one visitor tells the hiking blog Backpackerverse, before they encountered a wall of fog and heard scraping noises.

Even during the daytime the trail has sent chills through some hikers who insist the clouds take on skull shapes and that terrifying images materialize in the sands. Boulders are said to levitate, and shadow images flit about. Deeper into the forest area, some say the trees ooze a blood-red sap.

Although hardy hikers organize special haunted night treks, most of the regulars on this trail brush off these reports as no more than the results of overactive imaginations or heat exhaustion.

On weekends the trail can be packed with people on foot or bikes, and inconsiderate pet owners are the only things that scare most people. As one Yelp commenter noted: "Too many dog poops."

HIGBEE BEACH

They chased away the nudists
but not the spirits at the Jersey Shore.

Thomas Higbee died in 1879, but he didn't rest in peace. He was buried near the south New Jersey Shore hotel he operated. But when his heir, Etta Gregory, died in 1937, her will dictated that "Uncle Tom" be dug up and buried next to her in the nearby Cold Spring Cemetery in a grave filled with beach sand.

According to Craig McManus, a local medium, that's when the spectral visions started. "Perhaps Tom Higbee has never wanted to leave his old property overlooking the Delaware Bay," McManus told capemay.com. "Removing his body did not stop this ghost from continuing to walk the long stretch of the beach at night."

Higbee Beach Wildlife Management Area, now owned by the state, is known for these kinds of supernatural events, with reports of giggling and scratching noises from the dunes and strange visits from a pale man—sometimes wearing a long coat, sometimes in tattered pants held up with a sash.

Remote and beautiful, the beach attracts migrating birds—and the bird-watchers who photograph them—and for a time drew nude bathers, until then-Gov. Christine Todd Whitman signed a law in 1999 putting an end to that. Now, as *Weird NJ* magazine notes, "the only glowing body you might see on the Higbee Beach is that of a Higbee himself."

> ## "There have been stories of a ghostly man wandering Higbee Beach."
> *Coastal Living*

WATERSIDE SCARES
Eerie visions and spooky sounds roll in with the waves.

FORT STEVENS STATE PARK

The bones of a ship lie in the beach sands.

Through the thick fog in the early-morning hours of September 26, 1906, Capt. H. Lawrence of the 275-foot four-masted sailing ship *Peter Iredale* caught sight of the beacon from the Tillamook Rock Lighthouse.

Lawrence guided the ship and his crew of 27 toward the mouth of Oregon's Columbia River. But it was not plain sailing: Heavy winds during a fierce squall drove the ship onto a sand spit, and the force of the sudden stop snapped three of the vessel's masts.

The sailors escaped on a lifeboat sent from shore, and nobody was killed. A Naval Court inquiry commended the captain and cleared him of any blame. As his ship listed to the left, entombed in the beach, Lawrence gave her a final toast: "May God bless you, and may your bones bleach in the sands." Today, the skeleton from the *Peter Iredale* rises from those sands off what is now Fort Stevens State Park, a dramatic reminder of the power of nature over man.

Although it's an eerie spectacle, the wreck of the *Peter Iredale* has inspired no ghost stories. The same can't be said for the state park a few hundred yards away, though, the site of a Civil War fort that was put into action during World War II when the Japanese fired on it from the Pacific Ocean.

The spirit of an infantryman is said to patrol the abandoned Battery Russell, the other ramparts, the promenade and the campground. He appears to be wearing a World War II uniform, never speaks and seems skittish. Once he's sighted, he disappears.

WASHED UP
The *Peter Iredale* slammed into a sand spit during a squall.

SHENGSHAN ISLAND, CHINA

HOUTOUWAN VILLAGE

A remote fishing settlement on a Chinese island has been overtaken by vegetation.

Once a prosperous fishing village with a population of more than 3,000 residents, Houtouwan, on China's remote Shengshan Island, was deserted by many of its inhabitants in the early 1990s, who left for better schools and more reliable food sources. The village was officially depopulated in 2002, and as the years of abandonment continued, a blanket of lush vegetation overtook the cliffside houses.

As the climbing plants enveloped the empty houses and buildings, it created dramatic tableaux irresistible to photographers. When pictures went viral in 2015, people started flocking to the deserted town, creating a temporary crisis. "We urge visitors to preserve its tranquility for now," a local official pleaded. The pressure has since been relieved by viewing platforms and ticketed tours through the village.

A peek inside some of the homes reveals decaying household items, including bed frames and kitchen utensils. By 2018, about a dozen people remained in the village, selling water to tourists wandering the ghostly streets.

China's Other Ghost Towns

Almost 900,000 villages across China have been abandoned just in the 21st century, historian Feng Jicai told the *Jinan Daily News*. One of the most stunning is the town of Licha, which was built 800 years ago according to the principles of Taoism. It's been reported that it's now inhabited by just a single elderly couple, who regularly burn incense in the ancient temples to ward off evil spirits.

BROWNSVILLE, KENTUCKY

MAMMOTH CAVE

Get a supernatural poke in the ribs in this spooky National Park.

It would seem like the last place to put a hospital. Deep under Kentucky's Green River Valley run miles of pitch-black caverns with dripping stalactites and subterranean streams with blind albino fish.

But when Dr. John Croghan bought the cave for $10,000 in 1839, he saw this controlled, never-changing environment of constant 54 degrees to be the ideal spot to treat people for the killer respiratory disease of "consumption," today known as tuberculosis.

Inspired by underground hospitals in Europe he had read about, he brought in patients for experimental treatments in what would become a terrible medical miscalculation. Of the 15 first patients in the 11 huts built inside the cave, two died and the rest got sicker. By 1849, Dr. Croghan was also dead from TB.

Today, the failed "consumptive colony" is Mammoth Cave National Park, where the dead are said to return to shove and poke visitors when the lights are turned out. At Corpse Rock, where the bodies of patients lay before transport out of the cave, visitors have described hearing disembodied coughing.

Dr. Croghan also operated the cave as a tourist attraction, building the Mammoth Cave Hotel and using slaves as tour guides in the caverns. Stephan Bishop, a slave who was brought in as a teen and led tours up until his death in 1856, is buried in nearby Old Guide Cemetery. It's said his footsteps echo in the caverns he called a "grand, gloomy and peculiar place."

WHAT LIES BENEATH
The cave is the world's largest haunted natural place and has drawn tourists for two centuries.

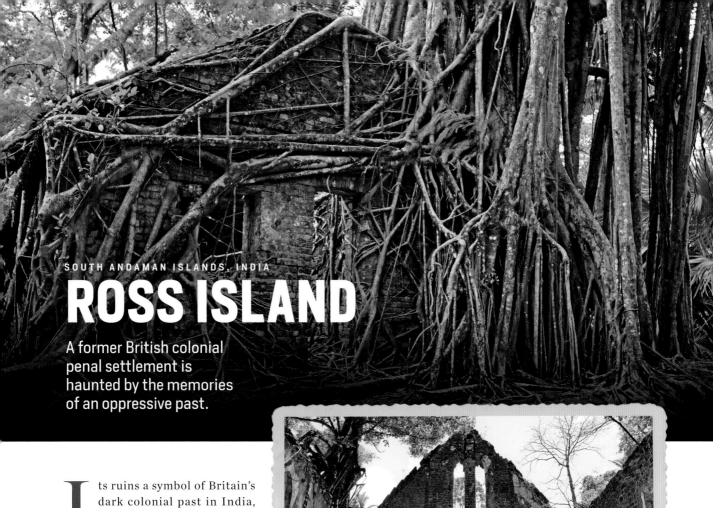

ROSS ISLAND

A former British colonial penal settlement is haunted by the memories of an oppressive past.

FORCED LABOR
Inmates were ordered to clear the forests and build bungalows, a church, tennis courts and swimming pools.

Its ruins a symbol of Britain's dark colonial past in India, Netaji Subhash Chandra Bose Island is a tropical ghost island in the Bay of Bengal. Formerly known as Ross Island, the island was named after a surveyor and once served as the headquarters and residences for a British penal settlement for Indians who mutinied against imperial occupation in the 1800s.

After uprisings on the mainland, convicts were shipped to barracks on neighboring islands in the Andaman Islands chain. With its isolation and high mortality rate from waterborne diseases, the British government spared no expense to attract administrators and their families to Ross Island, constructing grand ballrooms with teak dance floors, swimming pools, a tennis court, hospital, Presbyterian church and a water-treatment plant.

The island remained occupied by the British until 1942, when it was taken over by invading Japanese. In 1947, after India gained independence, it reassumed control of the then-abandoned island, with its buildings collapsing into ruins and the giant ficus trees reclaiming the land. Now, the only living remnants of colonial rule are the deer the Brits introduced as game animals.

137

YAMANASHI, JAPAN

SUICIDE FOREST

People hike into these dark and ancient woods determined never to come out.

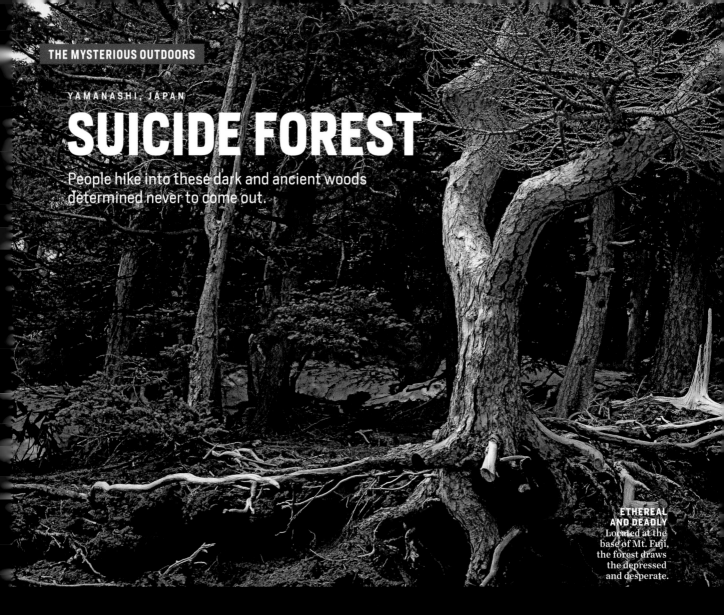

ETHEREAL AND DEADLY
Located at the base of Mt. Fuji, the forest draws the depressed and desperate.

As visitors enter the forest at the foot of Mount Fuji, they come across this warning sign: "Your life is a precious gift from your parents. Please think about your parents, siblings and children." Below, it gives the contact number for a suicide-prevention group.

A disturbing number of people visit Japan's Aokigahara Jukai, or Sea of Trees, find a secret place amid the dense groves of ancient gnarled trees that plunge the region into darkness even during the day—and decide to end it all.

As many as 100 people take their lives here each year, giving the ethereal forest the dubious distinction of being the most popular suicide location in Japan. YouTube star Logan Paul received widespread backlash in early 2018 for posting a video that featured a body still hanging from a tree amid the forest.

Some say people are lured to the forest by romantic notions of suicide depicted in novels set in Aokigahara. Others say visitors enter the woodland happy and healthy only to succumb to the shadows. Legends also tell of ghosts lurking behind tree trunks and rocks.

When somebody goes missing, the patrols spring into action. Most suicides are from hanging from the limb of a 300-year-old tree. Others are poisonings

GRIM DISCOVERY
Visitors have stumbled
upon remains of
suicide victims.

The Book of Death

In 1993, Japanese author Wataru Tsurumi published a controversial book entitled *The Complete Manual of Suicide*. An unlikely best-seller (it sold over 1 million copies), it recommended Aokigahara Jukai as a good place to hang yourself. Just one thing, the area was said to be haunted: Locals have reported often hearing the anguished cries of yurei— angry spirits—between 2 and 3 a.m.

or drug overdoses. Seventy to 100 bodies a year are retrieved for proper burial, and volunteers and locals constantly keep their eyes open for trouble.

"If I see someone on their own, I will go and talk to them," said Hideo Watanabe, a café owner who has saved 160 people over the years, to *The Japan Times*. "After a few basic questions, it's usually not so difficult to tell which ones might be here on a suicide mission."

OFFICIAL RESPONSE
Patrols began in 2009, looking for people at risk—often in vain.

139

BELGIUM

CHÂTILLON CAR GRAVEYARD

A 100-plus pileup was discovered deep in the European woods. How did the vehicles get there?

I t's a traffic jam that lasted for decades. Deep in a Belgian forest, more than 100 vintage American automobiles were lined up and left to rust in a haunting car graveyard whose history is as tangled as the roots invading the old chassis.

Some of the cars in this surreal site outside the small village of Châtillon were said to have been abandoned as far back as World War II. According to local lore, U.S. soldiers ditched their private vehicles in remote locations to hide them from invading Nazis. At war's end,

the Americans left many of their cars behind, rather than pay the high cost of shipping them home.

That may account for some of the cars, but not all, since many of them were built after the war. The later models likely came from Canadian employees of NATO living in Belgium and France after the war. They are believed to have bought them from a local garage specializing in selling and repairing American models, then had to leave them when they left France in the 1960s during the country's dispute with

NATO. The car graveyard was actually located on the land behind the garage.

Either way, the cars sat under the trees for years as locals stripped them—logos were particularly popular—and nature took its toll on what remained. Discovered by urban adventurers, the site became a popular destination due to the dramatic photos posted on the internet. The area drew unwanted curiosity-seekers for years. By 2009, locals—worried about the environmental damage from the cars—had cleaned up the area.

"The cars were driven up a hill, one by one, nicely parked and somehow hidden from the outside world."

AmusingPlanet.com

WHEELS UP
The auto cemetery is believed to have been one of several in Belgium.

141

TREES OF MYSTERY
Apparitions in the mist and electronic malfunctions are some instances of the paranormal activity.

FLYING SAUCER?
This 1968 photo purportedly shows one of the many UFOs attracted to the forest.

ROMANIA

HOIA BACIU FOREST

Locals call it the "Bermuda Triangle of Romania" for the sightings of ghosts and UFOs.

In the heart of Transylvania stands a small wood of crooked, ominous black trees. And in the heart of that grove is a ring of bare dirt where no plant has ever grown. Nearby vegetation shows strange signs of dehydration despite plentiful rainfall. Compasses are said to go haywire. All sense of time is lost. Headaches and nausea assault the body, and the skin erupts in burn marks and blisters. Eventually, the mind surrenders to primal fears.

Sometimes called the "Bermuda Triangle of Romania," the Hoia Baciu Forest got the reputation as the portal to the paranormal and jumping-off spot to other worlds. In the late 1960s, a military technician took a picture of what was supposedly a flying saucer over the 620-acre grove, providing what believers call photographic proof of the many UFO sightings before and since.

It's called the "Shepherd's Forest" after the story of a shepherd and his flock that disappeared seemingly into thin air. Locals these days seem to worry more about airsoft rifle shooters than evil spirits, based on the warning signs nailed to trees. Even the modern-day shepherds look unfazed as they guide their sheep through the trees safe and sound.

Camping is allowed, though for some visitors there is one aspect of the woodland that is truly frightening: There are no public restrooms.

POCOMOKE FOREST

The fictional Maryland forest of *The Blair Witch Project* has nothing on these real woods.

It seems every loblolly pine tree in this creepy forest has its own horror story, ready-made for the cinematic treatment. Consider the couple who ran out of gas one night in the dark woods of Pocomoke Forest, a real-life answer to the forest of terrors set in *The Blair Witch Project*. After the boyfriend went for help, leaving his girlfriend behind in the locked car, she heard scratching on the roof. Despite her terror, she fell asleep, then awakened the next morning to see her boyfriend's head on top of the car—he had been hung upside down from a tree and tried to get his girlfriend's attention by scraping the roof with his fingernails.

Countless tales like these are found in these 18,000 acres of swamp and uplands along the banks of the Pocomoke River, where otters frolic in streams and bald eagles soar high above the dogwood. Nighttime is said to stir up the scariest of the spirits, of the slaves who were beaten and raped by their owners who once controlled this land, of desperate farmers forced to give up their tracts during the Depression.

The woods play host to stories about an escaped killer from Cambridge State Hospital with a hook for a hand or about fireballs—could they be UFOs?—that cause cars to abruptly break down.

SCARY SIGHTS Spirits and perhaps a UFO emerge from the trees.

MONTSERRAT

PLYMOUTH

The capital city of a Caribbean island has been partially consumed by an active volcano.

For centuries, the Soufrière Hills volcano mostly sat dormant. Then, on July 18, 1995, the volcano stirred to life, belching ash and hot gas that blanketed the southern end of the Caribbean island of Montserrat, where the capital city of Plymouth was located.

As more volcanic matter rained down, residents were evacuated in December 1995 as a precaution. They were allowed to return months later, but a massive eruption in June 1997 that killed 19 people forced Plymouth's residents to flee again, many of them never to return to their island home.

The government sealed off the southern part of the island as an exclusion zone and the local economy, already hobbled by the devastation

decimated. More than half the island's original population of 13,000 is now gone, most to the U.K. (the island is a

stark and forbidding, encased in a thick, concrete-like mixture of lava, ash and rock, as the world's only capi-

LAYERS OF ASH
"Nowhere else can you see a buried city like the one we have here," volcanologist Rod Stewart told the website TripSavvy.

UYUNI, BOLIVIA

GREAT TRAIN GRAVEYARD

A violent past and a scary movie turn an
old government building into a maze of frights.

The Bolivian city of Uyuni draws tens of thousands of tourists each year as the gateway to the world's largest salt flats, a surreal barren expanse where the only structure is a hotel made entirely of salt. But just outside of town is another curious attraction.

The Great Train Graveyard, or Cementerio de Trenes, is the final resting place for early 20th-century locomotives and rail cars. Most of the more than 100 train cars were imported from Britain to link this trading post on the Andean plain with other South American cities.

The decline of the mining industry and disputes with neighboring countries doomed those dreams, and by the 1940s the trains were abandoned.

There are no guards at Cementerio de Trenes, so tourists climb on top of the engines corroded by the salty winds and take pictures inside the train cars, with one hull even converted into a swing.

"Most other countries would have removed the old trains, cordoned them off, or perhaps made a museum out of them," blogger Mike Powell wrote. "The fact that they've been abandoned here to be stripped by locals and climbed upon by monkey-like foreigners might not be the most constructive or safest idea, but it's pretty awesome."

HAUNTED FISHING SPOTS

Anglers may reel in trouble in these water holes with dark histories.

NEW YORK

POCANTICO RIVER

In this 9-mile-long tributary of the Hudson River in the outer suburbs of New York City, brown and brook trout swim the waters, eels navigate upstream in the spring —and *The Legend of Sleepy Hollow* runs deep.

Author Washington Irving had his Headless Horseman gallop along the banks of the Pocantico, seeking out victims. And while the frights come directly from fiction, the author found inspiration for his most famous short story in the region's many ghostly tales. One of those features the Headless Hessian—a Revolutionary War character thought to haunt Westchester County and attack unsuspecting locals near their homes.

EERIE TALES
Local legends inspired "Sleepy Hollow."

RED RIVER

It's a great place to fish, if you don't mind the witch. The Red River in Tennessee is the legendary home of Bell Witch, who was said to have resided in a cave near its banks in the 1800s, pestering the unfortunate Bell family. She unleashed beasts and sang annoying hymns at all hours. No less a figure than Andrew Jackson heard the tales, probably from Bell family members themselves, and sent out a patrol to find her, but the terrified soldiers refused to search. People still report sightings, including human shapes in the trees and, down there with the catfish and striped bass, all sorts of frightening creatures.

PESKY SIGHT The Bell Witch shares the river with the catfish.

WYOMING

PLATTE RIVER

When fog envelops the Platte River, the "Ship of Death" is said to appear, its masts crusted with frost; the crew, frozen ghouls. A trapper gets credit for the first sighting in 1862, and many others claim to have seen the ship until the early 1900s. If you're angling in these waters known for trout, you're safe, but a friend is not: Legend has it that on the deck lies somebody you know who'll be dead before the day ends.

WASHINGTON

GREEN RIVER

Steelhead and salmon populate the Green River, but so, too, do ghosts. Visions of women and girls are reported walking through and over the river. And no wonder: If you recognize this waterway's name, that's because it was attached to one of history's worst serial killers, Gary Ridgway, aka the Green River Killer, who terrorized this region in the 1980s and '90s. Once caught, he was given multiple life terms for 48 killings, although the number could top 100. That means many victims—most of them female hitchhikers and runaways—never got their day in court.

LOST & ABANDONED SITES

ONLY THE WIND, WEEDS AND GHOSTLY SOUNDS FILL THESE ONCE-BUSTLING LOCALES NOW LEFT ALONE.

MARBLE FALLS, ARKANSAS

DOGPATCH USA AMUSEMENT PARK

A hillbilly playground in the Ozarks slides into decay while clinging to hopes of a rebirth.

By 1967, hillbillies were hip. TV shows like *Green Acres*, *Petticoat Junction* and *The Beverly Hillbillies* topped the ratings. That's when ground was broken on Dogpatch USA, an Arkansas amusement park in the Ozarks inspired by the "Li'l Abner" comic strip.

The strip's artist, Al Capp, was so impressed with the 800-acre spread featuring a railroad, petting zoo, mill tour, trout pond and restaurant that would cook your catch that he said, "It's all so much more authentic that I'm going to change the comic to resemble this."

Although Dogpatch USA attracted respectable crowds and turned modest profits its first year, America's changing tastes, combined with Capp ending his comic strip in 1977 and competition from another outdoorsy park in nearby Branson, Missouri, sent Dogpatch on a slide longer and steeper than the park's Wild Water Rampage ride.

After changing owners several times, Dogpatch closed in 1993, leaving only a spooky and surreal world of broken-down slides, rusted amusement-ride cars, faded signs and collapsed buildings.

One of the only elements that still stands untainted is also one of the most eerie: the giant sculpture of "Kissin' Rocks."

But Dogpatch may have found a rescuer: In late 2017, a conservative Las Vegas–based entertainment company called Heritage USA agreed to lease the property.

Believing Christianity is under attack in America, the company says the park will be part of its mission to poke fun at Hollywood liberals, though the site's latest owner, Charles "Bud" Pelsor, told the Associated Press, "It will be a family-friendly theme park, not religious but family friendly."

PUCKER UP
(From left)
Dogpatch's creepy
"Kissin' Rocks"
sculpture;
only echoes
fill an abandoned
music hall.

"Everything is still here, it's just incredibly overgrown."
Owner Charles "Bud" Pelsor, to KOLR-TV

DOWNWARD SLIDE
Two personal-injury lawsuits compounded problems.

151

LIBERTY, NEW YORK

GROSSINGER'S RESORT

Goodbye, Liz Taylor. So long, Milton Berle. This once-swanky resort sits empty and rotting.

When summer bathed New York City in sticky heat, well-heeled residents during the post–World War II years fled for the Borscht Belt resorts of the Catskills. A two-hour car ride to the north, these vacation getaways, which rivaled the mob-run casino hotels of Las Vegas and Havana, offered comedy from Milton Berle and Jerry Lewis, swimming, golfing, hiking and (for the mostly Jewish clientele) kosher meals.

The jewel was Grossinger's Catskill Resort Hotel, a 1,200-acre, four-star vacation paradise that was the inspiration for the movie *Dirty Dancing*. Some 150,000 people a year streamed to the resort, which boasted its own post office and landing strip, two swimming pools, tennis courts and a golf course. Drinks flowed in the Pink Elephant Bar. Rocky Marciano trained here. Eddie Fisher, who was discovered at Grossinger's, would take both his wives—Debbie Reynolds and Elizabeth Taylor—to meet Jennie Grossinger, who founded the resort in 1914.

But by the late 1960s, cheaper airfares to Florida and Europe, air-conditioning that made the city tolerable in the summer, and baby boomers' changing tastes would doom the great resorts in the region. After Jennie passed away, her family sold the resort in the 1980s, but hopes for a casino license didn't materialize fast enough, and the place sat empty, left to scavengers, vandals and graffiti taggers.

"Peek over the fence and see something that looks like the set of *The Walking Dead*: rotted buildings, including decrepit hotel towers whose windows have been left open for decades," says Stephen M. Silverman, author of *The Catskills: Its History and How It Changed America*. "The shredded curtains behind them look like ghosts."

What the vandals didn't invade, nature did. Greenery enveloped the tennis courts, moss covered the walkways and sunlight streaming through the still-intact windows turned the massive natatorium into a sort of lush greenhouse. The Olympic-size pool now "morbidly curdles with globs of algae and subspecies of wildlife," says Silverman. "Elizabeth Taylor would not approve."

New Life Ahead?

After years of lying vacant, there may once again soon be swimming, golf and dancing on the grounds of Grossinger's. A 2019 agreement was reportedly made with Sullivan Resorts to demolish the property and build a $50 million hotel, including a golf course, convention center, spa, nightclub and more. No word yet if the ghosts of Borscht Belt past will stick around.

DEEP TROUBLE
A moldy pool symbolizes the abandonment of a luxury playground.

BIRMINGHAM, ALABAMA

SLOSS FURNACES

This once-mighty plant melted iron —and the occasional employee.

At the peak of its production, Sloss Furnaces ranked as one of the world's largest producers of pig iron, churning out 1,000 tons a day. The plant won a bronze medal at the Southern Exposition World Fair in 1883, and Birmingham was so prosperous it became known as "The Magic City."

This success came at a cost, however. In an era of little to no government workplace-safety regulations, Sloss employees were scalded by steam and melted iron, electrocuted, crushed by machinery, hit by railroad cars and poisoned by carbon monoxide.

"You actually had two men who were burned alive inside," historian Richard Neely told WIAT-TV. "We have a reputation that it seemed like people were dying every time you came out here." In all, about 20 workers were killed over the plant's 90-year history—considered an acceptable track record for the times.

This history of gruesome accidents has powered a number of ghost stories, establishing this now-abandoned plant as one of the most haunted industrial sites in America. Visitors report seeing the spirits of those maimed and killed ironworkers lurking among the old pipes or still toiling at their jobs, oblivi-

ous to the fact that they're dead and the plant is no more. Ghosts that can't be seen are said to poke and push people.

As with many legends, the stories about Sloss Furnaces have become more dramatic with each retelling. While pay was low and workers had to buy their goods at the company store, a Sloss job was considered a good one.

Building of the plant started in 1881, within a half-mile of rich iron ore deposits. Sloss became a smoke-belching symbol of America's industrial might after the Civil War. Management renovated the facilities to a state-of-the art level and oversaw aggressive expansion.

After reaching top production in the 1950s, Sloss slowed down, hampered by clean-air regulations and competition from overseas. It was finally shut down for good in 1970. Left empty, the plant became a rusty jungle of boilers and machinery, a symbol of a bygone era, but one that locals remember fondly.

Citizens passed a measure to stabilize the structures and build a visitors center. The Sloss Furnaces site received national landmark designation in 1981 and now houses a museum and metal-arts program. There are even nighttime ghost tours by lantern light around Halloween...if you're feeling brave.

DANGEROUS DAYS
Molten iron maimed
and killed employees.

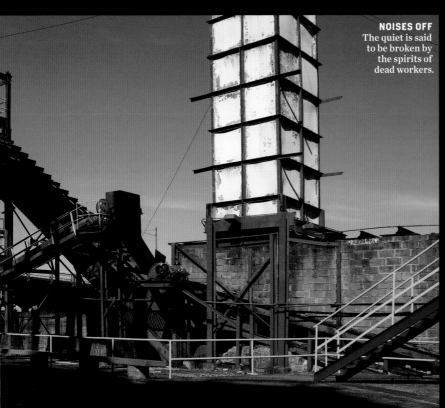

NOISES OFF
The quiet is said
to be broken by
the spirits of
dead workers.

"This was a
dangerous
place to work,
being scalded
by steam,
being splashed
by hot iron."
Historian Richard Neely,
to WIAT-TV

DYING OFF
With Detroit's own automobiles killing rail travel, the city's train station welcomed only vandals.

MICHIGAN CENTRAL STATION

Once a source of civic pride, Motown's train station now stands as a monument to despair.

The Michigan Central Station opened for commuter train service in 1914. The towering 18-story building was the tallest railway station in the world, with more than 200 trains departing each day carrying thousands of passengers.

This transportation shrine served Detroit well for decades. Reflecting the Motor City's success as a manufacturing powerhouse, the station welcomed Presidents Herbert Hoover, Franklin Roosevelt and Harry Truman and VIPs like Thomas Edison and Charlie Chaplin.

But ironically, it was the very popularity and success of the Detroit-built automobiles that doomed Central Station. Rail passenger service tapered off after World War II, and by 1967, the depot's shops and much of the waiting room were closed; only two ticket windows remained.

"No other building exemplifies just how much the automobile gave to the city of Detroit—and how much it took away," Dan Austin writes in the book *Lost Detroit: Stories Behind the Motor City's Majestic Ruins.*

The arrival of Amtrak in the 1970s brought a $1.25 million renovation, but the additional repair projects never got off the ground, hobbled by Detroit's sinking economy. And when Amtrak left the building in 1988, the stately station was shut down and left to ruin.

As vandals covered the walls in graffiti, tiles littered the floor beneath the crumbling marble archways and the windows on the office tower were punched out, opening the structure to the harsh Michigan weather. This former source of civic pride became a symbol of blight and despair. In 2009, the City Council approved a resolution to demolish Michigan Central Station. When preservationists sued the city, calling the station a historic landmark, the wrecking ball was canceled and modest renovations began.

In 2017, lights illuminated the station's windows for the first time since the 1980s as the building hosted a dinner for native Detroit business leaders to encourage them to "reengage and "reinvest" in Motor City.

Matthew Moroun, whose family trucking business purchased the building in 1995 and spent $12 million to begin renovations, including replacing all 1,050 windows, told the glittering gala that "today, demolition is unthinkable."

Plans now call for using the station for Amtrak trains, streetcars and a rail line to Detroit Metro Airport.

"Michigan Central Station is a symbol of Detroit's century of growth and decay."
NPR

FLYING HIGH
The entire building reportedly cost more than $11 million to construct.

KAZANLÂK, BULGARIA

COMMUNIST PARTY HEADQUARTERS

An otherworldly monument in Bulgaria looms atop a mountain.

High on Buzludzha Peak in central Bulgaria, where the winds hit gale force and temperatures drop to -13 degrees F, a group of socialists met in secrecy in 1891 to form the Bulgarian Social Democratic Workers' Party. More than eight decades later, local leaders commemorated the establishment of the forerunner to the Bulgarian Communist Party with a memorial whose bold architecture would match the dramatic setting.

Constructed by military workers and artisans, the Buzludzha Monument was a marvel of the Brutalist style of architecture, with steps leading up to a stout flying saucer–shaped hall constructed at the apex of a peak leveled with dynamite. Looming beside it was a 230-foot tower flanked in glass stars and topped with an observation deck accessible by elevator. The structure was used for Communist ceremonies, and Bulgarians who bankrolled its construction with

donations trekked to the peak to view glass mosaics of party heroes Karl Marx, Friedrich Engels and Vladimir Lenin, and allegorical images that included communist workers using their pitchforks to stab the serpent of capitalism.

After the collapse of communism in the late 1980s, the security guards were pulled away and the memorial suffered from the harsh elements as vandals stole the artwork and the valuable copper ceiling sheets.

IM COOLING TOWER

This imposing relic from a coal-burning power plant in Belgium looks like the belly of the Death Star.

For 86 years, the IM coal-fired plant in suburban Charleroi powered industry, warmed homes and kept the lights on for millions of people in Belgium. By the 1970s, as natural gas replaced coal, the plant, which was built in 1921, became the region's primary source of power, its massive water-cooling tower belching hot air to the heavens.

But when officials found out that the plant contributed 10 percent of Belgium's total carbon dioxide emissions, along with potentially infection-causing bacteria, protests erupted and the facility was closed in 2007.

Sitting empty, the complex was a local

ered it. The dystopian vision of curved terraces and long troughs filled with wild ferns beneath a giant hole to the skies delighted photographers, attracting a stream of visitors until the doors were sealed shut in 2017 for safety reasons.

STILL STANDING
Though slated for demolition, the tower that once cooled 480,000 gallons of water a minute

NEW ORLEANS, LOUISIANA

SIX FLAGS NEW ORLEANS

The Big Easy grapples with a major eyesore after Hurricane Katrina submerged these thrill rides.

When it comes to harrowing ups and downs, the rides at this Louisiana fun zone had nothing on the dizzying state of its finances. Opened in 2000 in New Orleans East, Jazzland Theme Park thrilled visitors with the Mega Zeph (a retro wooden roller coaster) and the Cypress Plunge log flume, plus a variety of other twisting, spinning rides and a merry-go-round.

The music ended for Jazzland after only two seasons when it went bankrupt, and the Six Flags group took over the 75-year lease. Upgrading the 140-acre park, Six Flags changed the name, imported thrill rides from its other parks and drafted plans for a water park to be included in the price of admission.

Then on August 29, 2005, Hurricane Katrina slammed into the Gulf Coast, flooding large swaths of New Orleans

when the levees broke. Overflow from Lake Pontchartrain submerged Six Flags under 20 feet of water, overwhelming the drainage pipes, knocking over buildings and exposing the peaks of the roller coasters in a vast lake of dirty water. Some coasters were damaged beyond repair; others dismantled and moved to different parks.

Once the floodwaters receded the

NOT FORGOTTEN
Scenes from *Percy Jackson: Sea of Monsters*, *Dawn of the Planet of the Apes* and *Jurassic World* were filmed at the park.

Flags said the costs of restoring the park were too high. The park was abandoned and sacrificed to the punishing Louisiana rains, a rusted-out ghost town of broken rides invaded by weeds.

Despite the many "No Trespassing" signs, urban adventurers still snuck through to explore. Various efforts to restore Six Flag fell through, and as residents complained, officials said they would look into demolishing the site.

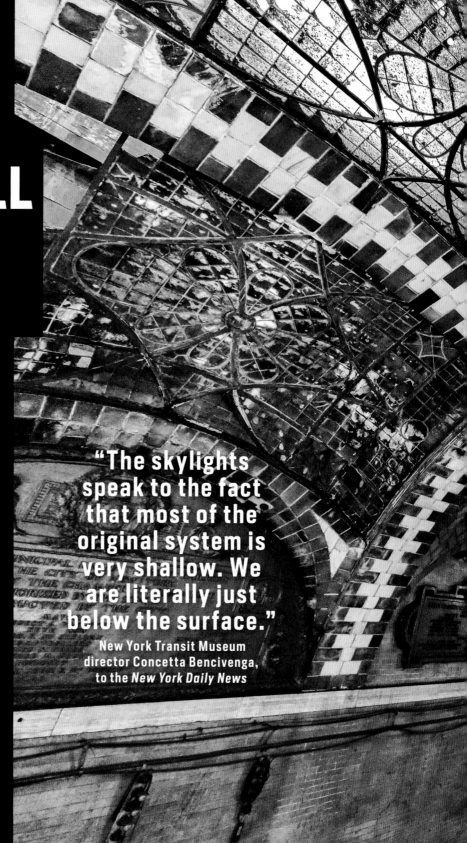

NEW YORK, NEW YORK

CITY HALL STATION

Manhattan trains don't stop at one of the most beautiful subway locations.

The subway stop beneath City Hall features the best in underground transportation amenities—a towering ceiling with skylights, colored-glass tiles, even brass chandeliers—everything, that is, except passengers.

Opened in 1904, the station became one of the least popular in the city, largely doomed by a problematic curving platform that limited the number of train doors that could be opened. In 1945, with only 600 passengers using the station each day, it was closed. Riders had to get off at the Brooklyn Bridge station and for decades they never saw this subterranean jewel.

While passengers still can't get off at the City Hall station, they can stay on the train as it swoops back uptown so they can get a glimpse of the Romanesque Revival architecture illuminated by sunlight streaming through the overhead glass. For an even better view, limited tours are offered through the New York Transit Museum.

"The skylights speak to the fact that most of the original system is very shallow. We are literally just below the surface."
New York Transit Museum director Concetta Bencivenga, to the *New York Daily News*

Not Quite Abandoned

While the old City Hall station is no longer a regular stop, it is still an active part of New York City's subway system. The number 6 local train uses the station's track as a turnaround point, screeching past the platform on its way back uptown about once every eight minutes, all day and night.

DETROIT, MICHIGAN

LEE PLAZA

A symbol of prosperity in the city becomes a boarded-up vacant apartment building.

To walk into the opulent Lee Plaza apartment tower when it opened in 1927 was to enter Detroit's optimistic state of mind. The 17-story art deco marvel featured everything a brash automobile-manufacturing powerhouse would want for its well-heeled residents—from the Peacock Alley main hallway with a hand-painted ceiling rendered in blues, greens and golds to the 220 luxury apartments (with chairs that would cost $12,000 today) to the on-site beauty parlor, flower shop, butcher, grocery store and library. Children could be left in a supervised playroom. A rooftop radio receiver ensured that every resident got the best reception. As a newspaper ad for the units boasted: "Every minor detail is attended to for a superior mode of living."

But the onset of the Great Depression in 1929, combined with the extravagant spending on the project, sent developer Ralph Lee into a financial tailspin. He had to sell the property not long after it opened and spent years battling with debt-holders, tying up the tower in court. Along the way, fancy residential apartments lost their allure to families who wanted free-standing houses, and the Lee Plaza had to take on renters instead of owners.

As the decline of its car factories sunk Detroit's local economy, the Lee Plaza lost its luster. By the end, the property that promised an "unmistaken atmosphere of refinement and taste" had become housing for low-income seniors. It was finally shut down in 1993.

Today, every window is boarded up and the elaborate plasterwork is crumbling into chalky piles on the dirty floors. The 50 decorative terra-cotta lion heads outside the building were stolen in late 2000, only to show up at another development in Chicago, prompting an FBI investigation. The expensive copper-tile roof was stripped away in the night, leaving gaping holes for Michigan's harsh weather to invade—and reducing the Lee Plaza, as historicdetroit.org observes, "from a towering symbol of wealth to a towering symbol of Detroit's decay."

"You wouldn't want to go wandering the corridors alone."
Journalist Toby Orton

NEW LIFE?
In 2019, the city announced plans to sell the building for use as affordable housing and a retail complex.

165

NOSE DIVE
Three years after the Olympics, Hitler drew the world into war, with the military taking over the village.

WUSTERMARK, GERMANY

BERLIN OLYMPIC VILLAGE

A symbol of Nazi might, the 1936 Olympic village faded into history after the Cold War.

Finding what he considered the perfect vehicle to promote Nazi propaganda and a nonthreatening image to the world in the first televised Olympics, Adolf Hitler supervised the construction of what he called the "village of peace" in the woods west of Berlin. The 4,000 male athletes from around the world for the 1936 Summer Games could relax between events in luxury dormitories with stewards, the first swimming pool in an Olympic village, and the three-story Restaurant of Nations dining hall in a complex designed like a typical German village, all located in Wustermark, Germany. (The 330 women who competed in the games were housed separately in quarters near the Olympic Stadium in Western Berlin.)

Behind the scenes, the athlete's village was hardly the idyllic hamlet as advertised, with the Gestapo monitoring phone calls and intercepting mail.

As the games began, the Führer's spin machine backfired when African American sprinter Jesse Owens captured four gold medals for the U.S., undercutting Hitler's claims of Aryan supremacy.

The village was built by the army, which just a few years later used it as a hospital and training academy during World War II, until the Soviets stormed into Germany and occupied the buildings in 1945.

The KGB developed torture and interrogation techniques in the village through the Cold War, until the facility was abandoned with the end of Communism in the 1990s. It's been left to rot ever since—the empty pool, the crumbling dining hall, the weed-covered buildings all reminders of its checkered past.

SARAJEVO OLYMPIC VENUES

The ski jumps, arenas and sled tracks in Bosnia and Herzegovina still show the ravages of civil war.

NEW THRILLS
The bobsled track on Mount Trebević (left) is occasionally used by extreme-bicycling competitors.

From the squalid aquatic center in Rio de Janeiro that helped anchor the 2016 Summer Games to Athens' weed-covered softball stadium from 2004, Olympic sites around the world betray the ravages of time, but none have suffered more than the venues in Sarajevo.

In 1984, the former Yugoslavia became the first Communist country and the first Slavic-speaking nation to host an Olympics with the XIV Winter Games in Sarajevo, the capital of what's now the modern day state of Bosnia and Herzegovina.

The city welcomed 1,272 athletes from a then-record 49 countries for 12 days of skiing, ice hockey, bobsledding, figure skating and speedskating before a worldwide TV audience in the hundreds of millions.

Then, eight years later, the fighting erupted. Three years of bloody civil war ripped the country apart. Sarajevo came under siege, with as many as 10,000 people killed. As troops took up positions in the surrounding mountains, the Olympic installations became battlements and artillery depots. Bullets tore into the bobsled track where Bosnian-Serbs had taken position. Some of the dead were buried in the Olympic arena.

Today, the city of Sarajevo continues to recover from those times, but the Olympic facilities still show the ravages of war. The concrete ski-jump ramps are collapsing into the hillside. The bobsled and luge tracks are scarred with graffiti, and moss covers the disintegrating audience stands.

BERLIN, GERMANY

SPREEPARK

A Soviet-era amusement park in Germany spirals out of control in a cloud of cocaine.

For the latter part of the Cold War, the only amusement park on either side of the Berlin Wall was the VEB Kulturpark Plänterwald, on the banks of the Spree river in Soviet-controlled East Berlin. Built by the communists in 1969, the Kulti, as locals called it, spread over 70 acres of blacktop with rides and attractions for all ages—some 1.7 million people a year—until it closed after the wall fell in 1989.

A reunified Berlin awarded a contract to overhaul the park to businessman Norbert Witte, who opened the newly christened Spreepark in 1991 with new rides, an English village, grass instead of hot asphalt around the Ferris wheel, and soon, a Disneyland-style single admission fee rather than separate fees for each ride.

After an initial bump in visitors, attendance slumped to about 400,000 people a year, and a debt-plagued Spreepark declared itself insolvent after going $14 million into the red. Witte fled to Peru with his family, close associates and six of his best rides—packed in shipping containers—in 2002. But trouble would follow the businessman who, in 2004, was sentenced to seven years in prison for trying a year earlier to smuggle nearly 400 pounds of cocaine from Peru back to Germany inside the masts of his Flying Carpet ride.

Spreepark, meanwhile, was forced to shut down, and the rides have decayed ever since, with marauders covering the buildings with graffiti and stealing whatever they can carry, and locals dumping trash.

"In the big hall there was a room, and it was absolutely filled up with Xerox machines....We were just like, 'What the hell?'" Tim Gärtner, project manager for Grüne Berlin, which owns the site, said in a 2018 interview with WBUR. The city has plans to restore the park, possibly using it to promote the arts.

TAKING OFF
"We don't have a lot of art in open spaces, in public spaces, like immersive art.... So it can be a very good place for that," project manager Tim Gärtner said of plans for Spreepark.

BIG WHEEL
Several of the
park's features
were destroyed
in a fire in 2014.

WILLIAMSBURG, VIRGINIA

PRESIDENTS PARK

A field of presidential busts goes bust in Virginia.

Geotge Washington has seen better days. His face is cracking and streaked with grime. Ronald Reagan fares even worse, having been struck by lightning. And let's not even get started on Abraham Lincoln, who has a poorly located hole in the back of his head.

Such is the state of the 20-foot-high busts of 43 of America's chief executives that once were arrayed in 10-acre Presidents Park in Williamsburg, Virginia. The statues were the creations of sculptor David Adickes, who drove by Mount Rushmore one day and was inspired to go 39 presidents better. The Virginia attraction opened in 2004, a year after a similar park was unveiled in Lead, South Dakota, complete with a Watergate picnic area near Richard Nixon's head and a seating area called Monica Rock near the Bill Clinton statue.

Presidents Park, which cost $10 million, never caught on with tourists, suffering from its obscured location behind a motel, and was forced to close in 2010. Three years later, the massive busts—weighing up to 20,000 pounds— were uprooted and transported by flatbed truck to a farm 10 miles away, where they were put into storage.

"The statues assume an entirely new level of creepiness under the evening skies."
Photographer John Plashal
to *Lonely Planet*

171

KUPARI, CROATIA

KUPARI RESORT

A former playground for elite soldiers in
Croatia betrays the horrors of war.

On some of the best beaches in the world stand the crumbling reminders of Croatia's bloody past. The seaside resort of Kupari dates back to 1919, when a Czech businessman built the Grand Hotel on the pristine waters of the Adriatic Sea in what was then the new kingdom of Yugoslavia.

By 1960, the country's military strongman, Josip Broz Tito, used Kupari as a resort for the military elite and their families, with four more hotels for 2,000 guests, along with villas and a campground. But during the Croatian War of Independence in the 1990s, the Yugoslav People's Army burned out all five hotels with phosphorus bombs, and locals scoured the ruins for anything valuable.

After the war, Croatia left the devastated shells of the hotels standing for decades as grim monuments, the only

DIM VIEW
"Nature has started to claim back the five hotels," *The Dubrovnik Times* observed. "In cavernous halls that once held fancy balls now grows ivy and weeds."

"guests" stray cats and vagrants. But with more tourists discovering the picturesque area near Dubrovnik, officials decided to tear down all but the Grand Hotel, with plans for it to be renovated and reopened.

CONSTANȚA CASINO

A gambling palace on the coast of Romania is destined for new life after decades of neglect.

From the outside, the Constanța Casino on the lapping waters of the Black Sea still shines as a blazing art nouveau masterpiece, where rich travelers visiting the Romanian Riviera gambled into the night in the early 1900s.

Commissioned at the turn of the 20th century by Romania's King Carol I and completed a decade later, the grand gaming house featured an auditorium with two billiard tables and 17 gaming tables for card games; it became one of the most popular casinos in Europe, even hosting Russia's doomed Imperial family in 1914. But its glory days were short-lived, as it followed the country's overall decline leading up to World War II. It served as a military hospital, was occupied by German troops and then was a restaurant for Communist leaders until it was closed in 1990.

Multiple plans to repair the casino have fallen through over the years, and the interior suffered from neglect, the chandeliered ceilings peeling and the floor tiles cracking—until officials crafted a two-year renovation plan set to begin in 2020 (work is currently in the design stage). A jubilant Constanța mayor exclaimed on Facebook: "Our casino will be rehabilitated and restored!"

BAD BET
The crumbling casino sits in the middle of a promenade, surrounded by well-maintained, upmarket buildings.

TAG SALE
The mall now is mainly used as a backdrop for movies like *Gone Girl*, TV's *Westworld* and Taylor Swift's music video for "...Ready for It?"

L ocal malls have taken a beating from their heydays in the 1970s and 1980s, due to the closures of large department stores and competition from online shopping. The Hawthorne Plaza in the Los Angeles suburbs had tried to carve out a niche by catering to middle-class residents who found such upscale centers as the South Bay Galleria, located to the south in Redondo Beach, too pricey.

But the 1-million-square-foot mall, opened in 1977 and covering six city blocks, suffered an additional economic blow with the loss of jobs in the surrounding aerospace plants. By the late 1990s, the 130 stores, plus the JCPenney, Montgomery Ward and Broadway anchors, were no more—and the mall closed its doors for good.

Officials are trying to find a use for the 40-acre site after a $500 million overhaul plan fell through in 2018. "We want to have development...but not at any cost," mayor Alex Vargas told the *Daily Breeze*. "We're not going to just have anything there if it isn't good for the city."

"[It's] creepy enough to make you think you're living in a George Romero horror movie."
Brian Champlin, We Like L.A.

DETROIT, MICHIGAN

PACKARD FACTORY

Wheels of change crushed this Michigan automobile plant, but hope is on the horizon.

Once upon an automotive time, the name Packard stood for luxury and American know-how, and the factory that churned out those cars reflected that commitment. Built from 1903 to 1911, the Detroit plant was a state-of-the-art manufacturing operation, with 4 million square feet spread over 40 acres and a force of 40,000 workers producing smooth-driving cars with such innovations as power steering.

When America entered World War II, Packard retooled to make engines for the P-51 Mustang fighter planes for the war effort, but struggled in the post-war 1950s to adjust to buyers' changing preferences for more modestly appointed cars. The last Packard rolled off the assembly line in the late 1950s, and the factory buildings were used mostly for storage before they were finally abandoned.

As Detroit's auto industry slumped, the plant became a rotting symbol of the city's lost economic glory days. Too expensive to renovate or even tear down, block after block crumbled, and the collapsed structures attracted vandals and squatters. Hollywood directors used the skeletal remains as backdrops for postapocalyptic scenes in TV shows and movies.

In 2013, Fernando Palazuelo, a Spanish businessman living in Peru, purchased much of the site for $405,000 with plans to renovate it, as he has with buildings in Spain, Nepal and Peru, into a $350 million residential, business, restaurant and retail center. "It will function like a mini city," Kari Smith, director of development for the project's site owner, Arte Express, told *The Detroit News*.

Sadly, the site's iconic bridge (right), though not part of the renovation plan, collapsed in January 2019.

GLOWING REVIEW
The buildings had large windows to bring in natural light, which the designer believed would make workers more productive.

Last Factory Man

Although deserted by Packard, the complex did not remain completely vacant. In 2019, Allan Hill, 74, was served an eviction notice to leave the abandoned graffiti-scarred warehouse. Hill had made the desolate building his home, and vowed to fight the move.

WASHINGTON

IRON GOAT TRAIL

A devastating avalanche still rumbles across the decades as the trapped and frozen victims yearn to be heard.

In 1910, a powerful snowstorm stranded the westbound Spokane Express passenger train and a smaller mail train at the Wellington Station, high in Washington's Cascade mountains, 70 miles from Seattle.

The higher the snow drifts grew, the more anxious the rail travelers became, until suddenly a monstrous avalanche hurled toward them, wiping out the trains and the entire station, and killing about 100 people.

What still stands as the worst rail disaster in American history prompted officials to rip out the tracks and abandon the tunnels in 1929 for a route at a safer lower elevation that is used to this day.

Now hikers can follow the old grade on the Iron Goat Trail, a 5.7-mile round-trip trek as breathtakingly beautiful as it is haunting, with chilling reminders of its horrific past, from the rusty cables to the decaying snow sheds.

In the decrepit snow tunnels, hikers swear they can feel the touch of invisible hands and hear the groans of the doomed "still trying to escape their tomb," according to hiking website backpackerverse.com. "Delve into these lightless corridors, but know you're not the only thing in there trying to find a way out."

SNOWED IN
(From left) The avalanche struck at the north end of this tunnel; rescuers found the victims buried in deep snow.

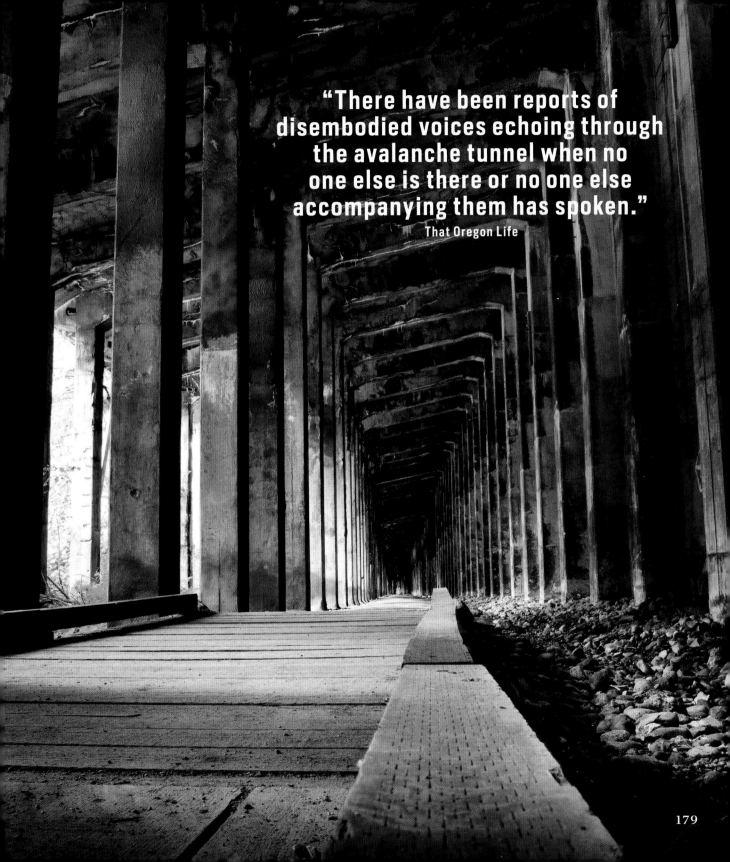

"There have been reports of disembodied voices echoing through the avalanche tunnel when no one else is there or no one else accompanying them has spoken."

That Oregon Life

KAMPOT, CAMBODIA

LE BOKOR PALACE HOTEL

A luxury French colonial resort in Cambodia with a violent history rises from the rubble.

Overlooking the Opal Coast of Cambodia, the majesty of Le Bokor Palace Hotel & Casino obscured its dark past. It opened in 1925 on a mountain considered sacred by Cambodians, and the lavish hotel served as a retreat for French colonists trying to escape sweltering Phnom Penh. The concrete art deco building was the centerpiece of a resort town, Bokor Hill Station, that also included a Catholic church and a post of-fice. For the dangerous construction project in this remote area, the French used Cambodian indentured servants, and an estimated 900 of them were killed during the work. In the 1940s, insurrections during the First Indochina War sent the French fleeing, and the hotel and other buildings sat empty until the early 1960s, when the resort was refurbished and operated for a decade, only to be abandoned again during the Vietnam War period.

For decades, the crumbling Le Bokor Palace Hotel stood on the mountaintop, sad and alone. But as modern roads were installed, more than 1 million tourists a year flocked to the area for both its scenic vistas and the temperate climate. While the Bokor Palace reopened as a luxury hotel in 2018, the eerie ruins of the nearby Catholic church and the rest of Bokor Hill Station still captivate those looking to revisit the past.

HIGH HOPES
Located 3,000 feet above sea level, Bokor was touted as a health resort, with claims that the salty, fresh air would cure fatigue, improve breathing, regenerate the blood and increase appetite.

BANGKOK, THAILAND

NEW WORLD MALL

Exotic fish now dominate a rainwater pool in a deserted shopping structure in Thailand.

An attempt at urban improvement resulted instead in the creation of a giant dirty fish tank at a former shopping center. The New World Mall in Bangkok welcomed shoppers from 1982 until 1997, when government officials determined that the developers had built more of the mall than they had permits for.

The mall was shut down and sat empty for years, with a fire in 1999 gutting the interior. In 2004, officials ordered the removal of the extra seven stories that the builders put up without permission, leaving the mall without a roof. Deep pools of rainwater led to an outbreak of mosquitoes, a problem people tried to solve by stocking the ponds with insect-eating koi, tilapia, iridescent shark, carp, mango fish and striped catfish. The mosquitos disappeared and the exotic fish population exploded, swimming around the old elevators. Some enterprising locals even sold fish food to visitors.

New World Mall still stands, but the government scooped up 3,000 fish and transferred them to less interesting waters throughout Thailand. A blogger for Nimbus Atlas visited the site and wrote in 2019 that "it felt like being in a Resident Evil-style/zombie apocalypse scene."

A TOURIST LURE
After photos of the mall fish went viral, the center was inundated with gawkers.

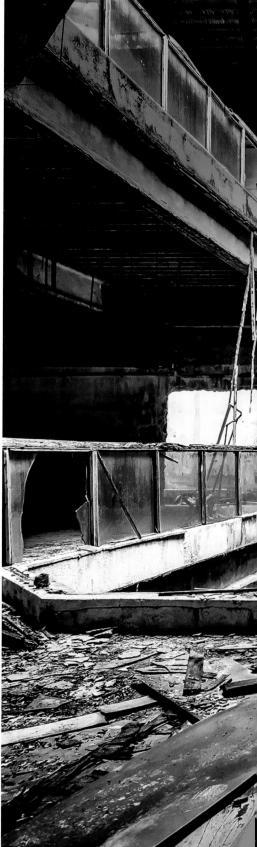

FISH TALE Schools of tilapia filled 5,000-square-feet of the mall's lower floor.

183

MILITARY MIGHT

Armed forces once hunkered down at these important outposts that now only fight the ravages of time.

THAMES ESTUARY, UNITED KINGDOM

MAUNSELL SEA FORTS

Set in the Thames Estuary on spindly legs like a Star Wars armored transport, the Maunsell Sea Forts helped defend Great Britain during World War II, with troops stationed on them shooting down 22 German warplanes crossing the English Channel and sinking one submarine.

Named after their designer, Guy Maunsell, the tower-forts were built on land and hauled out to sea, where they were affixed to concrete bases. Each tower housed as many as 265 soldiers on monthlong tours of duty. Equipped with guns, cannons and searchlights, the forts stood in the flight path of Luftwaffe fighters and "buzz bombs" heading toward London and other cities.

Decommissioned in the 1950s, the towers were used for pirate radio broadcasters in the 1960s and 1970s. Abandoned after that, all but a handful of the towers tumbled into the ocean.

ALSACE REGION, FRANCE
MAGINOT LINE BUNKERS

When the French constructed these concrete bunkers and artillery batteries along its border with Germany prior to World War II, they congratulated themselves on creating what they believed would be an impenetrable barrier that stretched 800 miles. But in 1940, the Germans crashed through a weak point to the north along the border with Belgium. Most of the fortifications were abandoned after the war and largely forgotten for two decades, until interest from military buffs and tourists prompted the government to open some bunkers for public viewing.

CRIMEA
BALAKLAVA SUBMARINE BASE

In Balaklava Bay, at the end of the Crimean Peninsula, a Soviet submarine base dug out in the 1950s was strong enough to withstand an American nuclear missile attack and deliver a retaliatory blow of mass destruction. To maintain secrecy, the surrounding town of 3,000 was virtually cut off from the rest of the world. After Crimea came under the control of Ukraine, the base was handed over to the military, then to Russia after annexation.

TUCSON, ARIZONA
AIRPLANE BONEYARD

After military planes fly their final missions, they usually wind up in a sprawling Arizona desert Air Force base, where they are stripped for parts and left to rest in peace. The technical name is the 309th Aerospace Maintenance and Regeneration Group, but everybody calls it The Boneyard.

With more than 3,000 craft from F-16s to helicopters to drones, this is the largest plane junkyard in the world. Established at the end of World War II, the facility has the planes neatly arrayed in a 2,600-acre parking lot, lashed to the hard, weed-covered ground to keep them from being swept away by winds. They remain in pristine condition thanks to the hot, arid climate, which prevents corrosion.

COVER Luuk de Kok/Shutterstock **FRONT FLAP** clockwise from top: Panther Media GmbH/Alamy; Fotolandia/Stockimo/Alamy (2); 1 Roger Viollet/Getty **2-3** Mmac72/Getty **4-5** Clockwise from bottom left: Jeff Hagerman/Media Drum World/Alamy; Toby de Silva; Roger Viollet/Getty; Courtesy Eastern State Penitentiary; Provost Kenneth/Media Drum World/Alamy; Michal Dziekanski/Getty **6-7** Kpzfoto/Alamy **8-9** Alan Lagadu/Getty **10-11** Clockwise from bottom: Stefano Montesi/Corbis/Getty (2); Wikimedia Commons **12-13** From left: Olivier Fay/Getty; Roger Viollet/Getty **14-15** From left: National Geographic Image Collection/Alamy; Geraldine Niva Johnson//Library of Congress **16-17** From left: Art Phaneuf/Alamy; Aaron Joel Santos/Alamy **18** From top: Courtesy bachelors-grove.com/Cobra97/Wikimedia Commons; Courtesy Hamilton Journal **19** From top: Kevin OConnell Photography/Alamy; Wikimedia Commons; Courtesy Ghost Research Society **20-21** Clockwise from left: Roberto Conte/Getty; Jim Dyson/Getty; Suzy Bennett/Alamy **22-23** Clockwise from bottom left: Bettmann/Getty; Karl Thomas Moore/Wikimedia Commons; Images-USA/Alamy **24-25** From left: Nat Farbman/The Life Picture Collection/Getty; Underwood Archives/Getty; Peter Stackpole/The Life Picture Collection/Getty **26-27** From left: MomoFotografi/Alamy; Jesse Ashenfelter/Shutterstock **28-29** Clockwise from left: Sergey Dzyuba/Alamy; Arcaid Images/Alamy; Boyd Hendrikse/Shutterstock; Mardiya/Shutterstock **30-31** Lightkey/Getty Clockwise from left: Bettmann/Getty (4); Donaldson Collection/Michael Ochs Archives/Getty **34-45** From left: Courtesy Eastern State Penitentiary (4) **36** From top: Courtesy Ohio State Reformatory; Photographs in the Carol M. Highsmith Archive, Library of Congress, Prints and Photographs Division **37** From top: Butski1977/Shutterstock; Wikimedia Commons **38-39** Clockwise from left: NY Daily News Archive/Getty; Media Drum World/Alamy; United Archives Gmbh/Alamy **40-41** From left: Matthew Christopher/Caters News; Will Ellis/Caters News 4**2-43** Courtesy Preston Castle (4) **44-45** Clockwise from top left: Courtesy Athens Asylum; Jerry Cooke/Pix Inc./The Life Images Collection/Getty (2); Jerry Cooke/Corbis/Getty (2); Jerry Cooke/The Life Picture Collection/Getty; Jerry Cooke/Corbis/Getty **46-47** Clockwise from left: Andy Drewitt/Newspix/Getty (2); Courtesy Aradale Lunatic Asylum **48-49** Courtesy University of Louisville Photographic Archives (6) **50-51** Clockwise from bottom left: Kurt Huebschmann/ullstein bild/Getty; Panther Media Gmbh/Alamy; Martin Sachse/ullstein bild/Getty (3) **52** From top: Media Drum World/Alamy; Alpha Stock/Alamy **53** Courtesy Catherine Morgan/Flickr (2) **54-55** Courtesy Dave Scaglione Photography (6) **56-57** Clockwise from left: Coug Kerr/Wikimedia Commons; Popperfoto/Getty; Courtesy Mythopolis Pictures **58-59** Eva Hambach/AFP/Getty **60-61** Clockwise from left: Elisa Rolle/Wikimedia Commons; Simon Webster/Alamy; Bradley Sauter/Alamy; Aydngvn/Shutterstock **62-63** NoSystem Images/Getty **64-65** Clockwise from bottom left: Burns Archives/Wikimedia Commons; Bettmann/Getty; Burns Archives/Wikimedia Commons; Bill Greene/The Boston Globe/Getty; Bettmann/Getty **66-67** Clockwise from top right: Terry O'Neill/Iconic Images/Getty; Bettmann/Getty; NY Daily News/Getty; Popperfoto/Getty; Bettmann/Getty; Police handout **68-69** Clockwise from left: Bettmann/Getty; Courtesy Suffolk County; Richard Drew/AP/Shutterstock; Paul Hawthorne/Getty **70-71** Courtesy of iaparanormal.com (8) **72-73** Clockwise from bottom left: Dax Ward Photography (2); Whitney Hayward/Portland Press Herald/Getty **74-75** Clockwise from left: Jeremy Woodhouse/Getty; Daniel Mihailescu/AFP/Getty; Stefano Bianchetti/Corbis/Getty; Stefan Cristian Cioata/Getty **76** From top: Courtesy Queen Mary; Imagno/Getty **77** From top: Artem Avetisyan/Shutterstock; Hulton Archive/Getty **78-79** From left: Rphstock/Alamy; Provost Kenneth/Media Drum World/Alamy **80-81** Clockwise from left: Domingo Leiva/Getty; Kpzfoto/Alamy; Fotolandia/Stockimo/Alamy (2) **82-83** From left: Boris Stroujko/Alamy; Cineclassico/Alamy; Edwin Remsberg/Getty **84-85** Clockwise from left: London Stereoscopic Company/Getty; The Print Collector/Getty; Leemage/Corbis/Getty

CENTENNIAL BOOKS

An Imprint of
Centennial Media, LLC
40 Worth St., 10th Floor
New York, NY 10013, U.S.A.

ISBN 978-1-951274-31-3

Distributed by
Simon & Schuster, Inc.
1230 Avenue of the Americas
New York, NY 10020, U.S.A.

For information about custom editions, special sales and premium and corporate purchases,
please contact Centennial Media at contact@centennialmedia.com.

Manufactured in China

Publishers & Co-Founders Ben Harris, Sebastian Raatz
Editorial Director Annabel Vered
Creative Director Jessica Power
Executive Editor Janet Giovanelli
Deputy Editors Ron Kelly, Alyssa Shaffer
Design Director Ben Margherita
Art Directors Andrea Lukeman,
Natali Suasnavas, Joseph Ulatowski
Assistant Art Director Jaclyn Loney
Photo Editor Keri Pruett
Production Manager Paul Rodina
Production Assistant Alyssa Swiderski
Editorial Assistant Tiana Schippa
Sales & Marketing Jeremy Nurnberg